SWIMMING HOLES
NEW ENGLAND

HELP US KEEP THIS GUIDE UP TO DATE

Every effort has been made by the author and editors to make this guide as accurate and useful as possible. However, many things can change after a guide is published—regulations change, facilities come under new management, and so forth.

We would love to hear from you concerning your experiences with this guide and how you feel it could be improved and kept up to date. While we may not be able to respond to all comments and suggestions, we'll take them to heart, and we'll also make certain to share them with the author. Please send your comments and suggestions to falconeditorial@rowman.com.

Thanks for your input!

SWIMMING HOLES
NEW ENGLAND

50 OF THE BEST SWIMMING SPOTS

Sarah Lamagna

FALCONGUIDES

ESSEX, CONNECTICUT

FALCONGUIDES®

An imprint of Globe Pequot, the trade division of
The Rowman & Littlefield Publishing Group, Inc.
4501 Forbes Blvd., Ste. 200
Lanham, MD 20706
www.rowman.com

Falcon and FalconGuides are registered trademarks and Make Adventure Your Story is a trademark of The Rowman & Littlefield Publishing Group, Inc.

Distributed by NATIONAL BOOK NETWORK

Photos by Sarah Lamagna unless otherwise noted
Maps by The Rowman & Littlefield Publishing Group, Inc.

British Library Cataloguing in Publication Information available

Library of Congress Cataloging-in-Publication Data

Names: Lamagna, Sarah, author.
Title: Swimming holes New England : 50 of the best swimming spots / Sarah Lamagna.
Other titles: Fifty of the best swimming spots
Description: Essex, Connecticut : FalconGuides, [2024]
Identifiers: LCCN 2023039627 (print) | LCCN 2023039628 (ebook) | ISBN 9781493076437 (paperback) | ISBN 9781493076444 (epub)
Subjects: LCSH: Ponds—New England—Guidebooks. | Hiking—New England—Guidebooks. | Trails—New England—Guidebooks. | New England—Description and travel.
Classification: LCC GB1816.3 .L36 2024 (print) | LCC GB1816.3 (ebook) | DDC 797.200974—dc23/eng/20231023
LC record available at https://lccn.loc.gov/2023039627
LC ebook record available at https://lccn.loc.gov/2023039628

Printed in Malaysia

Previous page: Bellevue Falls

For anyone who gets pulled to the wildness of water

CONTENTS

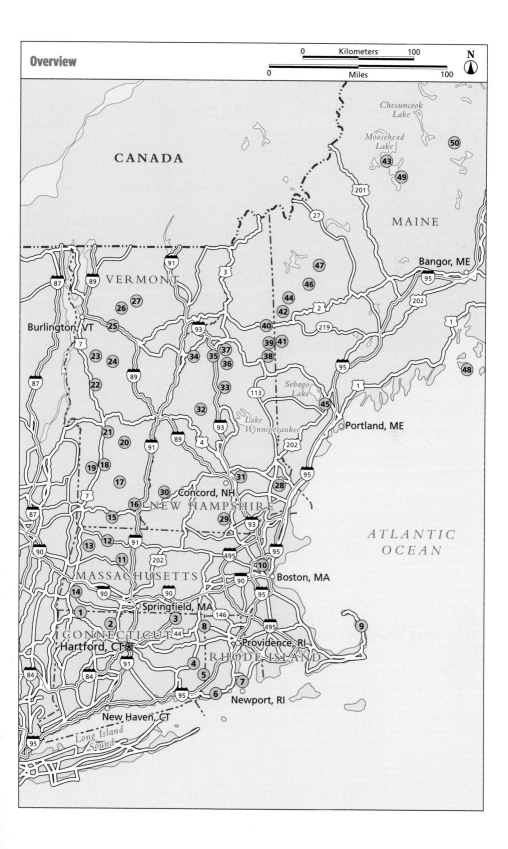

ACKNOWLEDGMENTS

First and foremost, I would not have been able to write this book without the support of my partner, Dan, who worked with my last-minute scheduling for all my watery adventures. Even though he travels frequently for his own work, he solo-parented without hesitation to help me out. But more importantly, thank you for always supporting my weird dreams and never questioning why I left a well-paid, solid career to make it work as a freelancer.

Thank you to my parents, who helped with a lot of the research for this book, including weathering crowded trails on holiday weekends. Thank you for bringing me into the wilderness at a young age to instill a lifelong love for the outdoors. Thank you for your undying support and love throughout all the chapters of my life.

Also, a huge thank you to my brother and sister for the incredible memories at Hammonasset Beach, Watch Hill, Hopeville Pond, and so many other places—including that one time we collected clams along the beach and stored them at our campsite, not knowing they would slowly decompose and stink up our entire pop-up camper.

Thank you to Holly Curtis and John Heinrich, as well as their kids, Curtis and Sunny, for having the terrible job of visiting one of the most remote swimming holes. I'm so sorry you had to spend a week on the mid-coast of Maine floating in solitude at Booth's Quarry while basking in the sun. It must have been torture for you.

An even deeper thank you to Holly, specifically, who has supported me in every instance since we met back in 2021. Your unending support is something I thought was only written about. You've shown me true friendship and I am forever grateful for it. While we're on the subject—Amy VanHaren, you are a gem of a human. You've taught me so many things this past year; most importantly, to believe in myself and the hard and amazing things I am capable of. I can never repay the guidance you've given me.

A big thank you to the private landowners who allowed me to enter their land and to add their swimming holes to this book. And to all the staff of the public lands I visited—you are the reason these beautiful lands are maintained for generations to come. Thank you for always answering my endless questions and being a force for good.

Finally, thank you to my son, Everett, who accompanied me on many of the swimming hole adventures. The laughter and wonder you brought to the wilderness filled my heart more than you know. I reflected on all the times I spent with my parents at the water's edge and how fondly those memories have stuck with me. I hope you will remember these days as ones when you were able to be wild and creative and happy. I am over-the-moon lucky to be your mama and will forever cherish these times we shared in some of the most beautiful places in the world.

MEET YOUR GUIDE

Sarah Lamagna is an ecologist-turned-freelance writer who spent most of her child-hood on the trails of New England. Her summers were spent on the coastal beaches of Connecticut and Rhode Island, where her love for water adventures bloomed. As she grew up, she developed thalassophobia—a fear of vast, deep, and often dark bodies of water. Because of that, she spent less time swimming in the ocean and, instead, sought more remote places to cool off.

She jetted off to college in upstate New York, where her love for wild water never ceased. One of the colleges she attended was on the banks of the Oswegatchie River, where she'd spend time studying for her exams while canoeing to private islands dispersed throughout the river.

Her partner's postdoc led them to the Rocky Mountains of Colorado, where she adventured throughout the Southwest. Sarah's thirteen-year career as an ecologist allowed her endless opportunities to be outside and immerse herself in nature. She specifically loved the alpine lakes found throughout the region after an arduous hike—the crystal-clear water was perfect for her phobia.

Motherhood brought different priorities to Sarah's life, and she became a full-time freelance writer. The autonomy, flexibility, and creativity of a freelancing career better suited her ability to parent and be present for her child. She moved her family back East to be closer to her loved ones, and to the wilderness she loved. Her writing focuses on adventure travel, ecotourism, and sustainability. She now lives in southern New Hampshire, where she is regularly seen swimming at the base of waterfalls or hiking up in the White Mountains, usually with her kiddo in tow.

INTRODUCTION

We New Englanders are hardy, adventurous souls, so it's no surprise that we not only hike up mountains but hike to our swimming holes, too. There's an extra piece of satisfaction when you dip your toes in the wild waters of New England after hiking through humidity, mosquitoes, and slick trails.

There are thousands of swimming holes across the region, but there's a rhyme and reason to the swimming holes I chose for this book. My first parameter was to disperse the swimming holes geographically and as equally as possible. Most of the swimming holes are inherently in the three northernmost states due to the abundance of wilderness compared to the southernmost states. And within each state, I tried my hardest to spread them all out, though sometimes I wasn't very good at this.

Another parameter I looked at was difficulty. Many swimming holes are tucked in the backcountry several miles into the wilderness—and I have a few of these in this book. However, I wanted to make sure that those who didn't want a huge hike still got to visit some beautiful swimming spots to relax in. So you will see a variety of distances and elevation gain throughout the book, with some locations just off the road.

And lastly, I wanted to have a mix of well-known spots that most folks (with a quick internet search) would already know about and also those that are a bit more off-the-beaten-path. I am a huge advocate for Leave No Trace principles, so no matter where you adventure, always remember to leave a place better than you found it.

The idea behind this book is to get you away from the beaches of New England (although you might find one or two amazing ones in this book too) and into the wilderness and along backcountry roads for a chilly dip in the clear waters of New England. The guide is meant to give you an idea of what to look out for when adventuring in New England, as well as some essential gear if your purpose is to go swimming.

HOW TO USE THIS GUIDE

Hiking to swimming holes is one heck of a fun time. I've been so busy working full-time and parenting my small child that I forgot how much I loved the wild waters of New England. This guide is meant to provide you with a range of hikes (and even some non-hikes) where the end goal is simply to swim in a swimming hole. There may or may not be big views spanning across mountains, and not every swimming hole is epic. But each of them is unique in its own way.

This guide is split up among the six states that make up New England: Connecticut, Rhode Island, Massachusetts, Vermont, New Hampshire, and Maine. I tried my best to ensure an even spread of hikes to cover all the corners of the region, but since New England covers a large amount of land, obviously, many areas are not covered. There is also the issue that backcountry swimming holes usually occur in the backcountry. Some states are inherently "wilder" than others and, thus, have more swimming holes.

Each swimming hole was chosen specifically with the goal that you want to swim at the end. In some cases, there are no trails to get to a particular swimming hole. Sometimes they're right off the road or the swimming hole is next to the parking lot. With that said, I tried to find a trail in the vicinity that you could explore prior to dipping in the swimming hole. I also did not want to assume that only one type of person would read this guide, so I wanted to have a range of difficulty for each swimming hole.

In addition to the trail beta (i.e., all the basic information for a trail) at the beginning of each hike, driving directions are also provided, starting from a major city close to the hike. You will also find step-by-step directions for the hike and what you'll encounter along the way.

THE BASICS

There are a few basic pieces of information at the beginning of each hike to ensure a safe and fun adventure for you and your group.

Start: the trailhead that you start from.

Elevation gain: how many feet of elevation gain you'll encounter. This is a huge deciding factor on how difficult a trail is, so keep this number in mind when deciding if a trail is right for you.

Distance: round-trip distance to and from the swimming hole in miles. This is another big factor in deciding the plausibility of a trail.

Difficulty: how difficult a trail is (see Difficulty Ratings section below).

Hiking time: how long it takes to hike a trail (see Hiking Time section below).

Fees and permits: how much it costs or if it requires permits (see Fees and Permits section below).

Trail contact: phone and address information of the management agency.

Dog-friendly: whether dogs are allowed on the trail.

Trail surface: what type of surface (e.g., gravel, dirt, boardwalk, etc.) you'll encounter.

Land status: who owns the land the trail resides on.

Nearest town: what city/town is closest to the trail.

Other trail users: if other trail users are allowed (e.g., horses, bikers, etc.).

Temperature of water: the average surface temperature.

Body of water: where the source of water comes from.

Water availability: if potable water is available.

Maps: maps that can be downloaded or printed prior to your adventure.

Toilets: if and where there are toilets available nearby.

Wheelchair compatibility: if strollers or wheelchairs can be used on any portion of the trail.

Family-friendly: whether the swimming hole (not the trail itself) has areas that are suitable for children.

DIFFICULTY RATINGS

This is one of the most subjective pieces of information that I provide in this guide. There are several factors that go into how strenuous it is to get to a swimming hole, including the ending elevation above sea level, the change in elevation throughout the trail, the length of the trail, and what hazards might be encountered along the way. I tried my best to standardize these difficulty ratings in the following categories:

Easy swimming holes are ones that are suitable for most hikers at any skill level. It includes swimming holes that are just off the road and take minimal effort to get to. Distances for these trails are usually capped at 2 miles with very minimal elevation gain (less than 300 feet). This category also usually includes trails that are stroller- and wheelchair-friendly, and will never require any rock scrambling or present many hazards.

Moderate swimming holes are suitable for those with a bit more experience in the outdoors, who are comfortable with longer distances and more elevation gain. These trails will likely range from 1 to 4 miles with no more than 1,000 feet of elevation gain.

Strenuous swimming holes are suitable only for those with more advanced experience on the trail. These trails are typically longer than 4 miles and usually have more than 1,000 feet of elevation gain (although not always).

HIKING TIME

This is another subjective piece of information that I provided. Hiking time varies with the skill level and overall stamina of the hiker. For most adults, the average hiking time is usually 2 to 3 miles per hour. For the sake of this guide, I conservatively estimated that most adults can do 2 miles in an hour, and the hiking times provided reflect that number.

FEES AND PERMITS

Depending on the management agency, sometimes fees and permits are required for entrance onto their land. Most state and national parks require a fee, and some of the more popular trails even require a timed permit to enter. Many times, the America the Beautiful National Park Pass covers more than just getting into national parks—it also covers parking in wilderness areas and land owned by the US Forest Service. In Connecticut, if you are a resident, all state parks are free when you drive your Connecticut-licensed vehicle into the park.

I have tried my best to accurately depict the types of fees that are required to park and recreate on the land the trail is on, but this is also something that can change quickly depending on the trail usage or political climate. Always call the local land management agency prior to your adventure to ensure you have what you need to get access.

Please adhere to the permitting and fee regulations to keep trails accessible to the public. The money collected from fees goes directly back to managing the land, whether that entails hiring more staff, maintaining trails and removing hazards, or simply buying trash cans to place at the trailheads. These management agencies are usually already severely understaffed and could use all the help they can get from our recreational use.

BEFORE YOU HIT THE TRAIL

Depending on your choice of swimming hole, there is a variety of preparations that must be made prior to an adventure. The following section gives the basic details of general hiking as well as considerations when swimming in backcountry waters. This section will also help you understand the importance of preserving these areas for generations to come.

TRAIL ETIQUETTE
There are some basic codes of conduct along the trail. Some of these are not hard-and-fast rules but more of a courtesy, and are always good to know prior to any hike.

RIGHT-OF-WAY
On most trails in the United States, the uphill hiker has the right-of-way. If you are like me, though, sometimes I need a break going uphill to catch my breath. The point is that the uphill hiker gets to decide whether they want to keep their pace.

Some novice hikers have a hard time wrapping their heads around this one, but there are distinct reasons why uphill hikers have the right-of-way.

1. Uphill hikers have a narrower field of vision and might not see folks coming down as quickly as those descending a trail can.

2. Uphill hikers have a harder time picking up their momentum again. Yes, downhill hikers might be going faster and have a harder time stopping; however, it's much easier for them to get going again after stopping. Uphill hikers must put in a lot more effort to get going again if they are abruptly stopped.

All this changes, though, when other trail users come into play. The general rule of thumb is that bikers yield to everyone, and everyone yields to horses. If, however, bikers are huffing it up the trail and come up behind you, it's just polite to step aside and let them pass.

Also, if you are a solo hiker and you come across a group of folks, it's generally good etiquette to let the group go by no matter if they are ascending or descending a trail. Making an entire group step aside can do a lot more damage to the edges of a trail than a single hiker.

DOG ETIQUETTE

This seems like a no-brainer, but please adhere to all leash laws. I cannot tell you the number of times someone has their dog off-leash and simply states, "Don't worry! My dog is friendly." At the crux of it, it doesn't matter whether your dog is friendly or not. There is a reason leash laws are put into effect, and it is on the trail user to know ahead of time what those laws are. For any of these swimming holes in the book, I let you know whether or not dogs are allowed.

Also, please pick up all feces from your pets while on the trail. This means not only picking up the poop and placing it in a doggie bag but also picking up the bag and throwing it out in a trash receptacle. Many trails on this list do not have garbage cans at the trailheads, so you need to pack out what you pack in. Do not leave bags on the trail for someone else to pick up.

DON'T FORGET TO KNOCK OFF THE DIRT

This is one of those things that people often forget or, perhaps, were never taught. Before you leave any trailhead after you have hiked the trail, check your gear for any mud, plants, or insects that might have caught a ride down the trail.

One of the easiest ways to spread non-native or invasive plant and animal species is through the soles of your hiking boots, the gear you carry, the clothing you wear, and the treads of your tires. So just do a quick check to make sure you aren't inadvertently giving anything or anyone a ride.

WIPE THOSE BODIES DOWN

When you are adventuring in the summertime (as you likely are if you have this book), you're going to have sunscreen and bug spray plastered all over you. However, at these backcountry swimming holes, those chemicals can do a lot of damage to a small body of water regardless of whether they are "reef-friendly." Wipe down your body at least 200 feet from the water source with biodegradable soap before you head into the pool.

STAY ON THE TRAIL

Again, this seems like a given, but please stay on the official trails. Trail erosion is a real threat to many of the trails in New England due to the sheer volume of people recreating on them. If trail users start making their own trails (called social trails), more erosion can take place.

In cases where there is no trail to reach the swimming hole, the best thing to do is wade the river until you reach the pool. Do not attempt to skirt the stream/river by walking along the water's edge. This can do irreparable harm to the area.

UNDERSTANDING TRAIL BLAZES

If you are new to New England, you might not have ever heard of a "trail blaze." Trail blazes are painted symbols (usually just a rectangle) on trees or rocks that show you the direction of the trail. Trail blazes are very common in New England and are how most trails are marked.

The general rule of thumb is that if you stand at one trail blaze, you should be able to see the next one up the trail, but that is not always the case. Also, if there are two blazes next to each other that are slightly offset, that means there is a turn in the trail. If the blaze on the right is higher on the tree than the left one, it means the trail goes right. If the blaze on the left is higher on the tree than the right one, it means the trail goes left.

Blazes can also be placed on solid rock when you are above tree line. This happens on many of the trails in New Hampshire, which tends to have a lot of solid granite trails. Rock cairns do not work as well in this state since wind and precipitation tend to knock them over.

LEAVE NO TRACE

There are seven basic principles to Leave No Trace—an organization dedicated to keeping the environment healthy while keeping trail users safe. For more in-depth information, feel free to head to the website: https://lnt.org. Here are the seven principles:

1. Plan Ahead and Prepare: Basically, know what you are getting yourself and your kids into. This hiking guide can assist in some of the logistics of planning ahead, but you also need to think of other things. Know the skills and abilities of all the people in your party, check weather, and have a backup plan.

2. Travel and Camp on Durable Surfaces: Like I said before, stay on the trail. This is what is meant by "travel on durable surfaces." But also, when you find a trail that opens up onto rock, stay as close to the blazes as possible and do not walk on the plant life that grows between rocks.

3. Dispose of Waste Properly: This one is fairly straightforward. Don't litter, and pack out what you pack in. This helps keep an area clean and also helps prevent wildlife from becoming nuisances on the trail.

4. Leave What You Find: This is the hardest one for those of us with kids. Children want to pick all the wildflowers and pinecones and rocks. Mistakes happen, of course, but there are ways to help prevent kids from picking up every little thing. I usually bring a toy (like a plastic car) for my kid to hold, or he uses one of my trekking poles to play "trail swords." Also, bubbles are a huge distraction in a pickle.

5. Minimize Campfire Impacts: If you don't need to build a fire, then don't. And if you do build one, make sure it's completely out before moving on. There is no need to start a wildfire because you didn't know how to properly extinguish a campfire.

6. Respect Wildlife: Do not pick up, aggravate, or try to pet any wildlife. Whether venomous snakes or harmless salamanders, please do not touch any wildlife for both your and their safety.

7. Be Considerate of Others: This is something you should think about in your life and not just on the trail. Common decency can go a long way on the trail, so just try to be a good person and a good trail user.

THE TEN ESSENTIALS OF HIKING

There are so many different types of gear that you could purchase in order to safely get outside, but I will not attempt to list all the options here. Instead, here are ten essential items of gear that you should always carry with you, no matter the size of your adventure:

1. **First-aid kit:** Any first-aid kit will do as long it fits the needs of your adventure. A longer adventure will need a more extensive first-aid kit.

2. **Navigation:** Either a GPS unit or a map/compass will do. You can use your phone, but always have backup navigation.

3. **Knife/Multitool:** There are great lightweight ones that easily fit in a small pack.

4. **Light:** A headlamp is best.

5. **Sun protection:** For swimming holes, avoid putting on sunscreen. Instead, wear SPF clothing and a hat.

6. **Water:** This seems obvious but needs to be stated.

7. **Food:** And not just some food but *enough* food for everyone.

8. **Layers:** For these hikes, you're going to be around water, so always assume that things will get wet and have backups.

9. **Fire:** Matches will suffice.

10. **Shelter:** It doesn't have to be a three-person tent, but at the very least carry an emergency bivy at all times.

THE ESSENTIALS OF SWIMMING

On top of the Ten Essentials, below is the list of items you should bring on a backcountry swimming adventure:

1. **Wear a bathing suit:** This might seem obvious, but still worth noting. Wear a bathing suit under your hiking clothes so that you don't have to change when you get to the swimming hole.

2. **Wear quick-drying fabrics:** This is especially useful if you don't plan to dry off completely before heading back from your hike.

3. **Use a quick-dry towel:** Rather than lug your heavy and clunky beach towel, invest in a good quick-drying one that easily packs down to fit in your backpack.

4. **Wear adventure sandals:** Brands like Chaco and Teva are good examples of sandals you can wear in and out of the water without hurting your feet. They also help with traction on slippery rocks.

HIKING SAFETY

Weather and Seasons

Anyone who has lived in New England knows how the weather and seasons change throughout the year. Winter can be brutally cold, summer is full of biting insects, and fall can have endless rain. Just because you are headed out on a hike doesn't mean Mother

Nature will keep the skies blue and the rain at bay. Always check the weather prior to any adventure, especially for those hikes above tree line. Storms can come in fast in places like the White Mountains and Baxter State Park. Always be prepared to turn around.

Ticks and Browntail Moths

Unfortunately, ticks and browntail moths are a regular part of outdoor life here in New England. They are pesky little buggers that are the bane of most hikers' existence. The best advice I can give you is to spray your gear with permethrin at the beginning of the season (always check the label, though) and use picaridin on your clothes and skin. I have never been a fan of DEET, so I try to stay away from it, but feel free to use DEET if you are comfortable putting it on your skin. Also, simply wearing long sleeves and tucking your pants into your socks works like a charm.

Poisonous Plants

There are several poisonous plants in New England, but the most common one found on the trail is poison ivy. There are a few trails in this guide where poison ivy is plentiful, so make sure you keep an eye on the trails when you hike. Again, wearing long sleeves and tucking your pants into your socks helps keep the dangerous oils off the skin and prevents irritation.

WATER SAFETY

Weather and Storms

Just like with any sort of hiking you do, always keep an eye on the weather. On the days leading up to an adventure, follow the radar and see what the trends are. If there is risk of significant rain or a thunderstorm, do not attempt to get into any water, especially moving water. Even if it isn't raining where you are adventuring, there may be rain and weather upstream from where you are. This can cause unexpected flash flooding, which could be deadly if you are caught swimming during that time.

It should also be noted that if water levels are high, do not attempt to swim in any moving water, especially if waterfalls are in the vicinity. No matter how good a swimmer you think you are, the current can be very strong and you'll be helpless against it.

Cold Water Immersion (Shock)

No matter what the temperature is outside, jumping into wild water can be a shock to your system. Sometimes it can be such a shock that a swimmer can get what's called "cold water immersion." It usually occurs when someone jumps into a body of water that is less than 60°F (although it can be higher than that too). The body is shocked by the dramatic change of temperature and the swimmer might start hyperventilating, which can lead to the swallowing of water and drowning. If you stay in long enough (often just a few minutes), your muscles might even stop responding, meaning you will no longer be able to swim, even if you are an excellent swimmer.

The best way to prevent cold water immersion is to wade into the water rather than jump or dive in. This is also a safer way anyway, since you'll get to know the layout of the swimming hole before you attempt to jump in.

Bacteria

Due to climate change and more intense storms and weather, there is a constant uptick in bacteria blooms throughout New England every year. During especially wet summers, toxic cyanobacteria thrive in the lakes, streams, and other bodies of water of New England due to the nitrogen- and phosphorous-rich runoff and erosion. Bacteria can cause skin irritation and gastrointestinal problems if you swim or wade in water infected with bacteria. It's best to avoid areas with unsafe levels of bacteria and wait for the water to clear.

You can check to see if there are any bacterial blooms in the area you want to go swimming by checking out that state's Department of Environmental Services. In popular public areas you may also see different-colored flags indicating if there are any warnings for that day (usually a bloom is signaled by a red flag).

Diving and Jumping

Even in the safest of places (i.e., a pool), diving and jumping into water doesn't come without risks. However, it gets even more risky in the backcountry. If it were up to me, I would argue that you should never jump or dive in any backcountry water ever. The risks are just too high. But if you insist on doing it, here are a few tips to make sure it's a safe experience:

1. Always heed signs and warnings put up by the management agency. If signs say you are not allowed to jump in, then don't. It's that simple.

2. Do some reconnaissance. If you're a paddler of any sort, you likely already do this. Basically, go into the water and see how deep the pool is, and what the bottom feels like. If the pool is too shallow, never attempt to jump in.

3. Inspect the rocks/cliffs around the pool. For those places that aren't as well-trafficked as others, the rocks/cliffs around the swimming hole might be covered in algae and moss, making for slippery conditions. All it takes is one wrong step and you could slip and hit your head.

Drownings/Fatalities

Sadly, drownings and fatalities happen every year in New England's waters. Many times, it's due to careless actions along the water's edge, leading to bumped heads leading to drownings or falls from high heights. Just because you don't think it will happen to you doesn't mean it won't. Always be aware of your surroundings, especially when around the swimming holes. Bring footwear with some traction (water shoes are great options) to help prevent slipping, and avoid areas that are unsafe due to bacteria, storms, or other types of weather.

MAP LEGEND

Municipal

≡(95)≡   Freeway/Interstate Highway

≡(202)≡   US Highway

≡(38)≡   State Road

≡[113]≡   County/Paved/Improved Road

———   Leader Line

Trails

------   Featured Trail

------   Trail or Fire Road

→   Direction of Travel

Water Features

⬭   Body of Water

∿   River/Creek

≋   Waterfall

Land Management

▢   National Park/Forest

▢   State/County Park

▢   Reservation Area

▢   National Monument/ Wilderness Area

Symbols

≍   Bridge

■   Building/Point of Interest

▲   Campground

▲   Campsite (backcountry)

†   Cemetery

×   Elevation

⌶   Gate

⊟   Inn/Lodging

▲   Mountain/Peak

🅿   Parking

≍   Pass/Gap

🎌   Picnic Area

🚻   Restroom

🔲   Scenic View/Overlook

○   Town

⑰   Trailhead

❓   Visitor/Information Center

🔲   Water

CONNECTICUT

Blue skies over Green Fall Pond

1 CAMPBELL FALLS

Connecticut might not be the first state you think of when it comes to wilderness, but you'd be surprised what the state has to offer adventurers. This watering hole sits in the northwest part of the state on the southern end of the Berkshire Mountains. It offers a dramatic plunge into a beautiful pool 50 feet below the top of the cascades.

Start: At the Yellow Blaze trailhead
Elevation gain: 140 feet
Distance: 1.0 mile out and back
Difficulty: Easy
Hiking time: About 30 minutes
Fees and permits: No fee required
Trail contact: Campbell Falls State Park Reserve, c/o Burr Pond State Park, 385 Burr Mountain Rd., Torrington, CT 06790; (860) 482-1817; https://portal.ct.gov/DEEP/State-Parks/Reserves/Campbell-Falls-State-Park-Reserve
Dog-friendly: Allowed on leash

Trail surface: Dirt, rocks/roots, and footbridges
Land status: State of Connecticut, Department of Energy and Environmental Protection
Nearest town: Norfolk, CT
Other trail users: None
Temperature of water: 65°F
Body of water: Whiting River
Water availability: None
Maps: Campbell Falls State Park Reserve map
Toilets: No
Wheelchair compatibility: No
Family-friendly: No

FINDING THE TRAILHEAD

From Hartford, take US-44 West for approximately 33 miles. Take a slight right onto CT-272 North/North Street for approximately 4 miles and then turn left onto Spaulding Road. After about 100 feet, turn right into the parking lot. The parking area can hold around 8 cars. GPS: N42 2.5398', W73 13.5876'

THE HIKE

Before anyone argues that this swimming hole is actually in Massachusetts, I'll be the first to admit that it's true. And although you can get to the swimming hole fairly easily from Campbell Falls Road in Massachusetts, the trail that starts in Connecticut offers a far better experience.

Start the trail along the Yellow Blaze Trail, although it's not marked with a yellow blaze very well. The trail, however, is very obvious and easy to follow. It starts off flat in the grass but quickly turns to dirt as you progress. There are a total of four footbridges along this trail, so tread carefully on rainy or dewy days, as these tend to get slippery.

You'll start to hear the falls a few hundred feet into the hike. As you get closer to the Massachusetts border, you'll see a stream that travels in the opposite direction of the falls. Do not follow this stream; instead, keep to the trail. There are markers on the trail when you reach the Massachusetts border, which means you're quite close to Campbell Falls. You'll see a small parking lot that can fit around two to three cars off Campbell Falls Road.

The trail starts to get steeper the closer you get to the falls. Once you arrive, you'll see what all the fuss is about. The waterfall plunges 50 feet into a tight gorge where the flow of water switches directions. The drastic change in flow offers a dramatic background to your swimming experience. There are several places you can jump in or simply wade in.

CAMPBELL FALLS

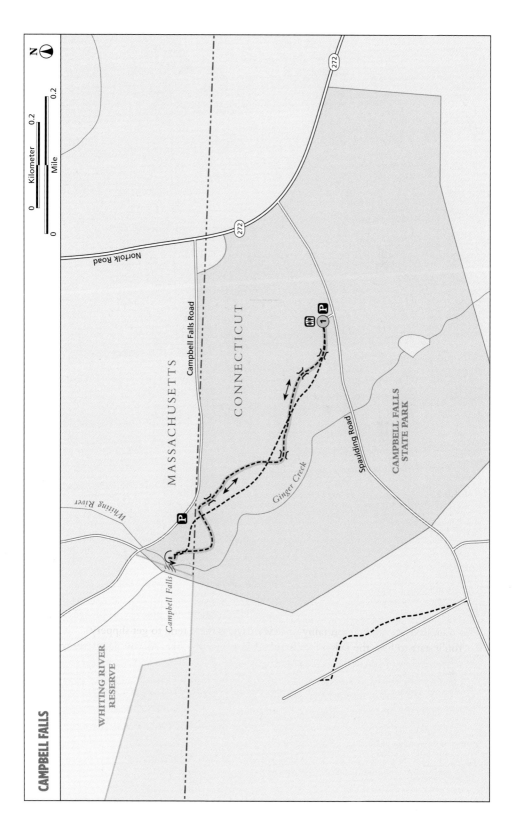

The serene swimming hole at the base of Campbell Falls

Looking downstream from Campbell Falls

MILES AND DIRECTIONS

0.00   Begin at the Yellow Blaze trailhead at the western side of the parking lot.

0.10   Encounter the first footbridge on this trail.

0.15   Cross over the second footbridge.

0.20   Cross over the third footbridge.

0.30   Cross over the fourth and last footbridge.

0.50   Reach Campbell Falls. Swim and then hike back the way you came.

0.70   Cross back over the fourth footbridge.

0.80   Meet and cross the third footbridge again.

0.85   Cross over the second footbridge.

0.90   Cross over the first footbridge.

1.00   Arrive back at the trailhead and parking lot.

WHAT IS GLACIAL TILL?

Thousands and thousands of years ago, the area that we call New England was covered in ice. As the glaciers retreated and our world warmed, the glaciers left a trail of rocks behind. This is known as glacial till—the unsorted material deposited by the movement of glacial ice. You can see evidence of this all over Campbell Falls State Park—from the fine sand and silt you see on the trails to the large cobbles and enormous boulders that line the water's edge. All the material found in the park and on the trail is around 15,000 years old and still changing to this day.

2 ENDERS FALLS

If you visit only one swimming hole in Connecticut, make sure it's this one. This is one of the most photogenic waterfalls in the state and is not to be missed. Enders Falls consists of five distinct cascades—the smallest is a 6-foot drop and the largest is a 30-foot horsetail. You can have your pick of pools to swim in when you hike to these incredible falls.

Start: At the Enders Falls trailhead
Elevation gain: 135 feet
Distance: 0.5-mile lollipop
Difficulty: Easy
Hiking time: About 30 minutes
Fees and permits: No fee required
Trail contact: Enders State Forest, Peoples State Forest, PO Box 1, Pleasant Valley, CT 06063; (860) 424-3200; https://portal.ct.gov/DEEP/State-Parks/Forests/Enders-State-Forest
Dog-friendly: Allowed on leash

Trail surface: Gravel, wood stairs, and platform for viewing
Land status: State of Connecticut, Department of Energy and Environmental Protection
Nearest town: Granby, CT
Other trail users: Hunters
Temperature of water: 65°F
Body of water: Enders Brook
Water availability: None
Maps: Enders State Forest map
Toilets: Yes, at the trailhead
Wheelchair compatibility: No
Family-friendly: No

FINDING THE TRAILHEAD

From Hartford, take I-91 North for approximately 10 miles. Use the right 2 lanes to take exit 40 toward Bradley International Airport and continue for 3 miles. Take the exit for CT-20 West toward East Granby/Granby. Merge onto CT-20 West and drive for approximately 5.5 miles. Take the slight left to continue on CT-20 West for another 3.4 miles. Turn left onto CT-219 South for 1.4 miles until you reach the public parking lot on the left. The large parking area can accommodate around 40 cars. GPS: N41 57.2946', W72 52.7394'

THE HIKE

There are several trails that lead from the parking lot and head down to the falls, but the main trail is obvious on the southwestern side of the parking lot. Start the trail next to the port-a-potty and begin your descent. The trail is a wide, gravel path that quickly leads to a spur trail. Take this spur trail to view the first set of falls—a 6-foot cascade. Get back on the main trail and keep heading down until you reach a fork. Here you'll veer right, down a set of stairs, to reach the second of the waterfalls—a 30-foot horsetail and plunge waterfall with dramatic gorge walls on either side. This is a popular spot for fishing.

Keep heading down along the stream and you'll find more sets of stairs and more waterfalls—it's a common theme throughout this short hike. The third falls are the most popular, and for good reason. The way the water cascades down the ledge and then switches direction makes for an extraordinary photo. This is a great option for a pool to swim in, but be aware that this place can get crowded with folks wanting to take photos of the falls.

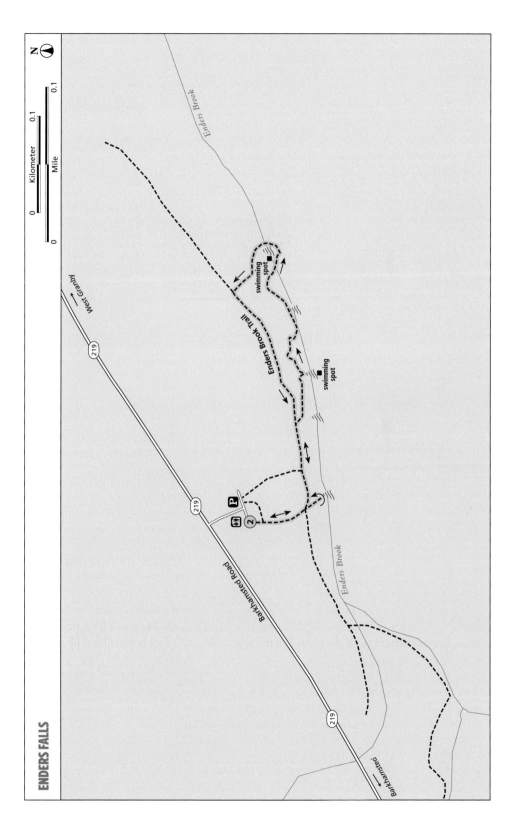

ENDERS FALLS

The third set of
waterfalls

The fourth set of waterfalls isn't as beautiful as the third or fifth, so I'd keep moving if I were you. The fifth set of waterfalls is considered two separate segments and drops 15 feet into a smaller (but still swimmable) pool. This is the best option for those wanting to take a little plunge, as it is likely less crowded than any of the other waterfalls (many visitors opt to turn around at the third falls).

You can continue going the same direction on the trail since there are just a few sets of stairs to get back up to the main trail. You can also head back the way you came to get a glimpse of all the waterfalls again.

Part of the trail to Enders Falls traverses stone steps

The third set of waterfalls and a great option for swimming

MILES AND DIRECTIONS

0.00 Begin at the trailhead on the southwestern side of the parking lot.

0.05 Stay straight on the short spur trail to see the first set of falls. Go back to the main trail and veer slightly right. Swimming is okay here but not the best.

0.10 Veer right at the fork and climb down the steps. You'll see the second set of waterfalls in front of you.

0.15 Pass the second set of waterfalls (popular fishing spot) and see the third set of falls (the most photogenic and beautiful pool to swim in).

0.20 Fourth set of waterfalls (not photogenic but a good pool to swim in).

0.25 Fifth set of waterfalls with a great pool to swim in.

0.30 Hit the main trail again. Go left to go back to the parking lot.

0.45 Veer right to follow the gravel path back to the parking lot and your car.

0.50 Arrive back at the trailhead.

3 BREAKNECK POND

In what is called the Last Green Valley lies the beautifully serene Breakneck Pond within Bigelow Hollow State Park. This area of Connecticut is surprisingly rural and is called the Last Green Valley due to its lush land with little to no artificial light. The dark night skies and abundant ecosystems allow wildlife to thrive in the area, which is easily seen within the park. Most visitors head to the boat launch at Bigelow Pond to dip their toes in the water, but venturing north to Breakneck Pond awards hikers with gorgeous views and solitude on the water.

Start: At the White Blaze/East Ridge trailhead
Elevation gain: 225 feet
Distance: 6.0-mile double loop
Difficulty: Moderate
Hiking time: About 3 hours
Fees and permits: Fee required; free for CT residents
Trail contact: Bigelow Hollow State Park, 298 Bigelow Hollow Rd., Union, CT 06076; (860) 684-3430; https://portal.ct.gov/DEEP/State-Parks/Parks/Bigelow-Hollow-State-Park-Nipmuck-State-Forest
Dog-friendly: Allowed on leash
Trail surface: Dirt and rock

Land status: State of Connecticut, Department of Energy and Environmental Protection
Nearest town: Union, CT
Other trail users: Mountain bikers and hunters; foot traffic only on Blue Blaze/Nipmuck Trail
Temperature of water: 75°F
Body of water: Breakneck Pond
Water availability: None
Maps: Bigelow Hollow State Park map
Toilets: Yes, at the trailhead
Wheelchair compatibility: No
Family-friendly: Yes, with supervision

FINDING THE TRAILHEAD

From Hartford, take I-84 east for 30 miles. Take exit 73 toward Union and turn right onto CT-190 East for 2 miles. Then turn right onto CT-171 East for 1.4 miles until you see the entrance for the park on your left. Drive on the park road until you reach the East Ridge trailhead parking on the northern tip of Bigelow Pond.

From Norwich, take CT-32 North for 9 miles and then turn right onto CT-203 North. Continue on CT-203 for 5.3 miles, then turn right onto US-6 East for 2 miles. Turn left onto CT-198 North for 12 miles and then turn left onto CT-171 West for 5.4 miles. The entrance to the park will be on your left. Drive on the park road until you reach the East Ridge trailhead parking on the northern tip of Bigelow Pond. GPS: N41 59.8968', W72 7.5198'

THE HIKE

This trail is one I know well and have traveled on often. My mother brought me here as a child, and this was our go-to hike on a hot summer day. The trail starts across the road from the parking area at the White Blaze/East Ridge trailhead. After just 0.25 mile, go right at the first junction to head on the No Blaze/Forest Road Trail. At the next junction, stay left to continue on the No Blaze Trail. At the next junction head left to go north onto the Blue Blaze Trail toward Breakneck Pond.

BREAKNECK POND

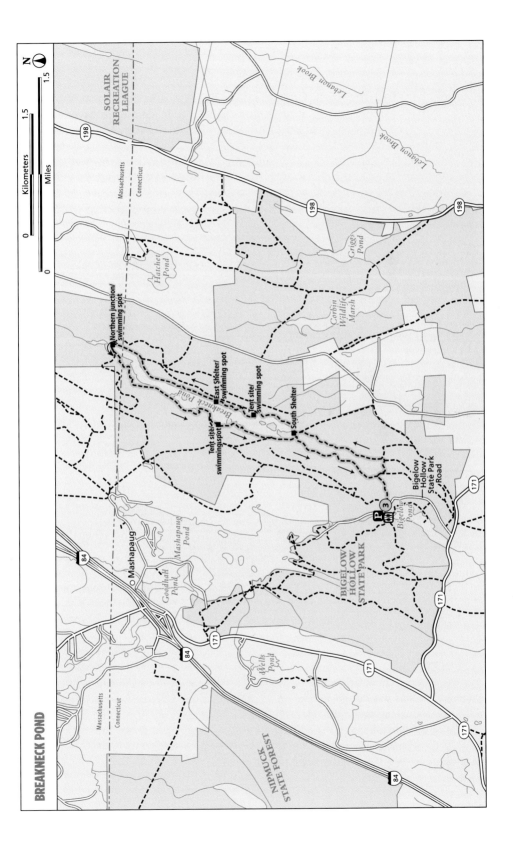

NIPMUCK STATE FOREST

BIGELOW HOLLOW STATE PARK

SOLAIR RECREATION LEAGUE

Massachusetts
Connecticut

Massachusetts
Connecticut

Lebanon Brook

Lebanon Brook

Griggs Pond

Corbin Wildlife Marsh

Hatchet Pond

Northern junction/ swimming spot

East Shelter/ swimming spot

Breakneck Pond

Tent site/ swimming spot

Tent site/swimming spot

South Shelter

Bigelow Hollow State Park Road

Bigelow Pond

Mashapaug Pond

Mashapaug

Goodhall Pond

Wells Pond

N

Kilometers
0   1.5

Miles
0   1.5

The area has high beaver activity, which you can see along the trail

The Blue Blaze Trail is wide and flat and spits you out at the southern tip of Breakneck Pond after a 0.75-mile walk. When you reach the southern tip, head right toward the eastern side of the pond, where you'll pass a lean-to on your left. You can hang out here if no one is camping there—to catch your breath or take in your first views of the pond.

At 0.5 mile past the first lean-to, you will reach a camping area along the water's edge. Leave No Trace principles tell us that you should always camp 200 feet from water, but this is already an established site and can be used to camp. This is also the same area where it's easiest to get in the water. There is a large rock right at the water's edge, so you'll know you're at the right spot.

If someone is camping here, please do not disturb their area; instead, wade into the water farther down the trail. About another quarter mile down the trail, still heading north, you will reach a second lean-to site (called the East Shelter). This is another spot where you can easily get into the pond. As with the other spots, please do not disturb guests who are set up in the area to camp.

FIRST-TIME BACKPACKERS

Breakneck Pond is a perfect place to dip your metaphorical toes into the world of backpacking. If it has ever intimidated you to carry everything you need for a few nights in the backcountry on your back, use this trail to ease into the sport. The South Shelter lean-to is only 1 mile from the trailhead, with very little elevation gain. It doesn't require slogging over miles of trail to set up camp, so if something goes wrong, you can head back to your car easily. If you're feeling more ambitious, you can also hike to the second shelter or one of the backcountry tent sites along the pond.

Get back on the trail by heading toward the northern tip of the pond. When you reach the three-way junction, take the trail all the way to your left and follow the blue blazes with the white dots in the middle to make your way down the western side of the pond. If you want to dip into the water before heading home for the day, the northern tip is another great spot to wade in.

Eventually, you'll arrive back at the junction at the southern end of the pond. There is a lot of beaver activity along the western bank of the pond, so be on the lookout for the little critters. It can be cumbersome to navigate the trail due to them regularly clogging up the culverts in the area.

Take the first junction on your right to head down the White Blaze/Park Road Trail and back toward your car. End the trail by taking a right onto the White Blaze Trail, where you'll meet back up at the northern tip of Bigelow Pond. You can dip into Bigelow Pond if you're still aching for some water time. Just be on the lookout for scuba divers, who regularly use this pond to train.

MILES AND DIRECTIONS

0.00 Begin at the White Blazes/East Ridge trailhead at the northern tip of Bigelow Pond.

0.25 Turn right on the No Blaze/Forest Road Trail and then almost immediately stay left on the No Blaze/Forest Road Trail.

0.35 Turn left onto the Blue Blaze/Nipmuck Trail.

Breakneck Pond stretches
through Nipmuck State Forest

A view of the pond from the trail

1.10	Arrive at the southern tip of Breakneck Pond and the South Shelter. Stay right at the junction to follow the eastern side of the pond.
1.50	Arrive at the tent site and first swimming spot.
1.80	Arrive at the East Shelter and a second swimming spot.
2.75	Meet up with the Blue–White Dot/Breakneck Pond View Trail. At this point, other trail users like horses and mountain bikers can use the trail along with hikers.
2.95	Stay left at the three-way junction to continue on the Blue–White Dot/Breakneck Pond View Trail. Or wade in once again at another swimming spot.
4.10	Arrive at the established backcountry campsite right at the water's edge.
4.85	Arrive again at the South Shelter and the southern tip of Breakneck Pond. Take the first right after rounding the tip of the pond and hike the White Blaze/Park Road Trail back toward your car.
5.70	Turn right off the Park Road Trail and continue on the White Blaze/East Ridge Trail.
6.00	Arrive back at the trailhead.

4 HOPEVILLE POND

If you're looking for a family-friendly swimming option in Connecticut, look no further than Hopeville Pond. This state park has a campground, a beach area, and plenty of hiking trails for little legs. But it also has the remoteness that you want when searching for a good backcountry swimming hole. Bring plenty to eat and drink, since you'll likely spend all day here.

Start: At the Hopeville Park trailhead (south of the main swimming area)
Elevation gain: 30 feet
Distance: 1.3-mile loop
Difficulty: Easy
Hiking time: About 45 minutes
Fees and permits: Weekend/holiday fee for nonresidents; free for CT residents
Trail contact: Hopeville Pond State Park, 929 Hopeville Rd., Griswold, CT 06351; (860) 424-3200; https://portal.ct.gov/DEEP/State-Parks/Parks/Hopeville-Pond-State-Park
Dog-friendly: Allowed on leash on trails and at picnic areas; prohibited on the beach
Trail surface: Dirt and gravel

Land status: State of Connecticut, Department of Energy and Environmental Protection
Nearest town: Griswold, CT
Other trail users: Cyclists
Temperature of water: 75°F
Body of water: Hopeville Pond and Pachaug River
Water availability: At parking lot and throughout the campground
Maps: Hopeville Pond State Park map
Toilets: Yes, at the trailhead and in the campground
Wheelchair compatibility: Some of the trail is on paved road.
Family-friendly: Yes

FINDING THE TRAILHEAD
From Hartford, take CT-2 East for approximately 36 miles. Take exit 28N to merge onto I-395 North toward Providence. Follow I-395 North for approximately 10 miles, then take exit 24 for CT-201 toward Hopeville. Turn right onto CT-201 and follow for 1.4 miles until the split in the road. Take the right fork; the park entrance will be on your right about 0.5 mile down the road. Parking is plentiful, with over 100 spaces for cars as well as a small overflow lot. GPS: N41 36.4302', W71 55.5864'

THE HIKE
Once you park at the beach parking lot, keep your beach gear in your car until after the hike—and believe me, you don't want to miss out on the hike. But make sure you wear your swimsuit, because there's a less-visited area of the park where you can take a dip in the river before heading to the beach.

Start the trail just south of the beach. Unfortunately, the trail is not blazed, but due to the high foot traffic, it's easy to follow. You'll meander through the large white pines on the property and along the water's edge. The trail is dotted with sweet pepperbush, pink azaleas, and American hazelnut. Some of the trees have some misshapen trunks that look like troll legs edging out toward the water.

The trail forks around 0.3 mile from the trailhead. Go right, and soon you'll reach a footbridge to cross over a small stream that feeds into the Pachaug River. At this point,

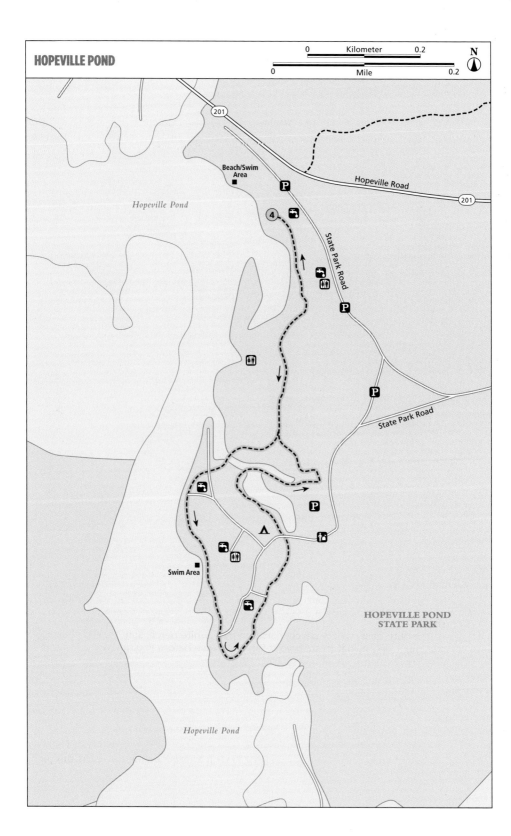

HOPEVILLE POND

0   Kilometer   0.2

0   Mile   0.2

N

201

Hopeville Road

201

Beach/Swim Area

Hopeville Pond

State Park Road

State Park Road

HOPEVILLE POND STATE PARK

Swim Area

Hopeville Pond

The trail passes old-growth white pine trees that look like they have feet

you'll head into the campground area of the park. Keep taking rights along the road around the campground to stay as close to the water's edge as possible.

At about the 0.5-mile mark, you'll reach a small beach that many campground guests use but hardly any day-use visitors do. Once you've had your fill of the water, head back on the trail to loop around the other end of the campground to end up at your car and the main beach once again.

WHY NOT BRING YOUR FISHING POLE?
In case you get tired of swimming for hours, bring your rod to try your hand at fishing. Hopeville Pond and the Pachaug River entice many anglers to their shores to find some great fish to bring home for dinner. Common fish include largemouth bass, yellow perch, northern pike, white perch, sunfish, and chain pickerel. Don't forget to snag your fishing license before you go!

MILES AND DIRECTIONS

0.00   Begin at the trailhead on the southern end of the main beach area.

0.30   Cross over a footbridge to head to the campground.

0.50   Come to a small beach area; feel free to take a dip in the water.

The swimming area at the pond is perfect for a family day at the beach

0.90 Cross over another footbridge to get back onto the trail you took at the beginning of the hike.

1.30 Arrive back at the trailhead. Grab your beach gear from the car to head back to the main swimming area.

5 GREEN FALLS AREA

No matter your adventure style, the Green Falls Area of Pachaug State Forest has it all. Not only is it at the junction of three of the longer trails in the state, but it also offers swimming (of course, this is a swimming holes book), kayaking/canoeing, camping, waterfalls, glacial fields, mill ruins, and even a ravine. It truly is a nature playground that you should check off your list.

Start: At the Blue/Orange Blaze trailhead
Elevation gain: 90 feet
Distance: 1.8-mile loop
Difficulty: Easy
Hiking time: About 1 hour
Fees and permits: No fee required
Trail contact: Pachaug State Forest, Rte. 49, PO Box 5, Voluntown, CT 06384; (860) 424-3200; https://portal.ct.gov/DEEP/State-Parks/Forests/Pachaug-State-Forest-Green-Falls-Area
Dog-friendly: Allowed on leash
Trail surface: Dirt, rocks/roots, and boulders

Land status: State of Connecticut, Department of Energy and Environmental Protection
Nearest town: Voluntown, CT
Other trail users: Mountain bikers and hunters
Temperature of water: 70°F
Body of water: Green Fall Pond
Water availability: None
Maps: Pachaug State Forest map
Toilets: Yes, at the trailhead and in the campground
Wheelchair compatibility: Not on trails, but picnic and swimming areas are accessible.
Family-friendly: Yes

FINDING THE TRAILHEAD

From Norwich, take I-395 North for approximately 7 miles. Take exit 22 for CT-164 toward CT-138/Preston City/Pachaug. Turn right onto CT-138 East for approximately 6 miles. Take a sharp right onto CT-165 West/CT-49 South and then quickly make a right onto CT-49 South. Continue on CT-49 South for approximately 2 miles and turn left onto Fish Road. Follow this dirt road for approximately 1 mile until you reach the parking area, which can hold about 40 cars. GPS: N41 31.971', W71 48.6492'

THE HIKE

Of all the swimming holes in this guide, the one that brings back the most memories is Green Fall Pond. Growing up, I never knew what to call it—Green Falls, Green Fall Pond, Green Falls Area—it went by many names. Officially, the pond is in the Green Falls Area of Pachaug State Forest, and it is one of the most beautiful ponds in the state. I remember endless days spent swimming in this body of water with friends, trying to reach the rock in the middle of the pond.

The trail starts at the parking lot and loops around the entire pond. Feel free to go either way, but for this guide I suggest right so that the pond is always on your left. Follow the Blue/Orange Blaze Trail for the entirety of the hike. You'll keep close to the water's edge almost the whole time, with many spots to take in the views of the pond.

At just under a mile, you'll reach the dam and subsequent waterfall. This is also where you'll reach the junctions of two long trails: the Nehantic and Narragansett. (If you want a good backpacking trip, either of these trails is a good option.) For a real treat, head

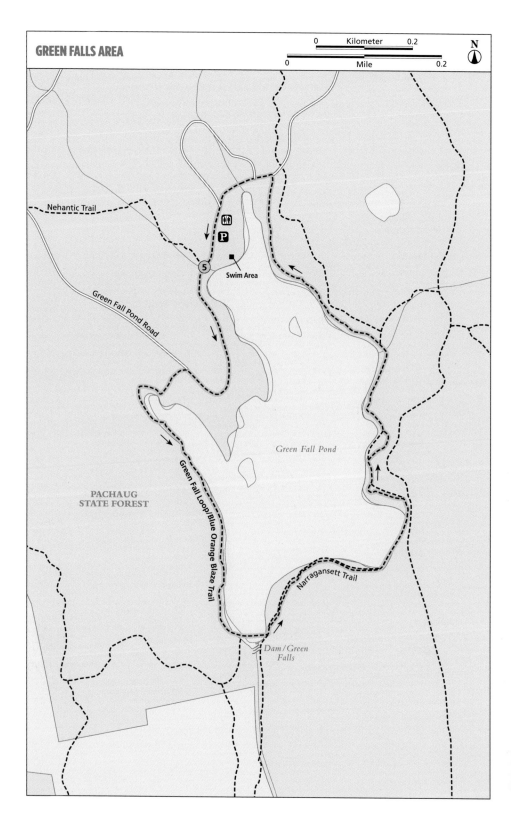

GREEN FALLS AREA

Kilometer
0   0.2

Mile
0   0.2

N

Nehantic Trail

P

5

Swim Area

Green Fall Pond Road

PACHAUG
STATE FOREST

Green Fall Pond

Green Fall Loop/Blue Orange Blaze Trail

Narragansett Trail

Dam / Green
Falls

right down the Blue Blaze Trail into a ravine (see sidebar). Once you're done checking out the ravine, hike back toward the waterfall and continue on the Blue/Orange Blaze Trail.

The trail continues along the pond's edge, where you might see ducks and geese floating on the water. You'll reach a fork in the trail around the 1.5-mile mark. Veer left to again stay close to the water. When you reach the 1.6-mile mark, you'll find huge

A picnic table sits at the pond's edge for those needing a little break

A quiet and serene swimming hole

One of the beaches along Green Falls Area

boulders just off trail that are split down the middle. Keep heading on the Blue/Orange Trail to make your way back around to your car and enjoy the swimming hole at the parking lot.

MILES AND DIRECTIONS

0.00 Begin at Blue/Orange Blaze trailhead that starts at the parking lot. Go right so that the pond is on your left.

0.85 Reach the junction with the Narragansett Trail on your right. Continue straight across the dam. Green Falls will be off to your right.

0.90 Continue on the Blue/Orange Blaze Trail, which will parallel the Narragansett for a little while.

1.45 At the fork, stay left to continue along the water's edge.

1.60 Reach huge split boulders.

1.80 Arrive back at the trailhead and swim area.

A forested trail leads the way
to Campbell Falls

RHODE ISLAND

A view from
the trail in Fort
Wetherill State
Park HOLLY CURTIS

6 LITTLE NINI POND

Are you tired of having to choose between a beach with a lifeguard and the open wilderness? Luckily for you, Ninigret Park has the best of both worlds. Little Nini Pond lies in the middle of the massive Ninigret Park, which houses several other recreational activities, too. But the park is also next to the Ninigret National Wildlife Refuge, where you can walk along the water's edge to view the migratory bird species the area is known for.

Start: At the Grassy Point trailhead
Elevation gain: 15 feet
Distance: 1.2 miles out and back
Difficulty: Easy
Hiking time: About 30 minutes
Fees and permits: No fee required
Trail contact: Ninigret Park, 4540 S. County Trail, Charlestown, RI 02813; (401) 364-1200; https://charlestownri .gov; and Ninigret National Wildlife Refuge, c/o Rhode Island National Wildlife Refuge Complex, 50 Bend Rd., Charlestown, RI 02813; (401) 364-9124; www.fws.gov/refuge/ ninigret
Dog-friendly: Off-leash dog area within the park; dogs prohibited at wildlife refuge
Trail surface: Paved, dirt, grass, and rocks

Land status: Town of Charlestown and US Fish & Wildlife Service
Nearest town: Charlestown, RI
Other trail users: Cyclists in the park; foot traffic only within the wildlife refuge
Temperature of water: 75°F
Body of water: Little Nini Pond
Water availability: Throughout the park
Maps: Ninigret National Wildlife Refuge map
Toilets: Yes, at the playground and wildlife refuge parking lot
Wheelchair compatibility: On paved roads within the park; none in wildlife refuge
Family-friendly: Yes

FINDING THE TRAILHEAD

From Providence, take I-95 South for approximately 13 miles. Keep left at the fork to continue on RI-4 South, following signs for North Kingstown. After driving for around 10 miles, continue straight onto US-1 South for approximately 18 miles. Make a U-turn and then immediately take a slight right onto RI-1A South for about 1 mile. Turn left onto Park Lane and drive to the parking area. GPS: N41 21.8946', W71 39.3732'

THE HIKE

You don't have to choose between playing some tennis, cycling, sunbathing at a sandy beach, or walking in the wilderness when you check out Little Nini Pond. I suggest starting your day at the wildlife refuge, especially if you get there early in the morning when the birds are waking up and ready to start their day.

Begin the hike from the parking lot, going straight toward the water. When you hit the junction of the trail, veer left to head north. At the 0.2-mile mark, you'll reach the northernmost point of the trail, which juts out into Ninigret Pond. Continue south on the trail.

Around 0.5 mile along the trail, you'll reach a junction. Stay straight and then at the next junction, go left to head toward the overlook area at the end of Grassy Point. You'll

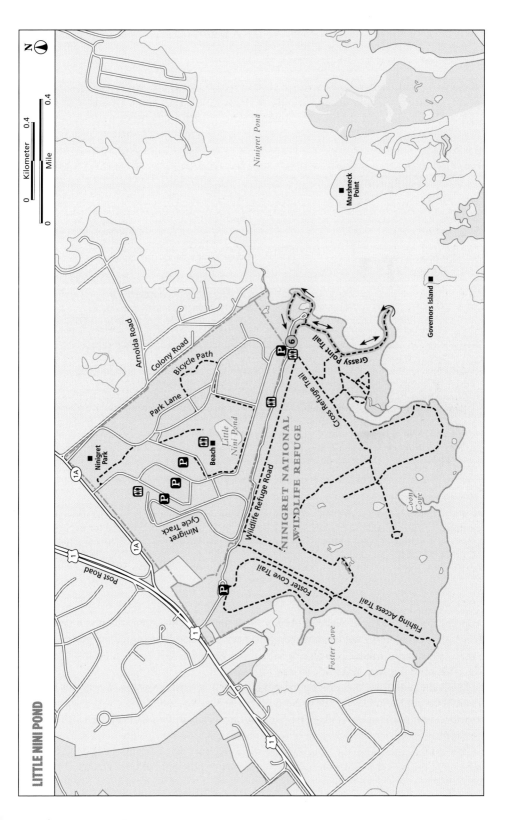

LITTLE NINI POND

N

| 0 | Kilometer | 0.4 |

| 0 | Mile | 0.4 |

Post Road

Arnolda Road

Colony Road

Bicycle Path

Park Lane

Ninigret Park

Little Nini Pond

Beach

Ninigret Cycle Track

Wildlife Refuge Road

NINIGRET NATIONAL WILDLIFE REFUGE

Foster Cove Trail

Fishing Access Trail

Foster Cove

Coon Cove

Cross Refuge Trail

Grassy Point Trail

Ninigret Pond

Marshneck Point

Governors Island

6

reach the end after walking about 0.7 mile. Don't forget to bring your binoculars on this hike so you can scope out the migratory birds in the area. But if you did forget them, there is a viewing scope at the end of Grassy Point for you to use at your leisure.

When you've soaked up all the birdcalls and the smell of the ocean, head back the way you came. When you meet a junction, turn right and then at the next junction, take a left instead of continuing straight from where you came. This will lead you away from the water and back to the parking lot. From here, you could walk to Little Nini Pond, which is just north of the wildlife refuge. Simply take a left onto Park Lane and follow it around

THE CUTEST SHOREBIRDS YOU HAVE EVER SEEN

You might hear a common shorebird while you're adventuring around Ninigret Park. You may even see them. A protected species called the piping plover is one of the most adorable shorebirds you'll ever see. They remind me of a wind-up toy, scurrying about on the beach trying to get their food. But where exactly do they get the name from?

The sand-colored, black-eyed birds have what most scientists describe as a "plaintive" call. Their mournful cries echo along the beach and are easily heard before the birds are ever seen, which is why they are called piping plovers. If you see them, please keep your distance and do not disturb them (that means refraining from chasing the birds). Piping plovers are a threatened species in the Northeast (they're endangered in the Great Lakes region) and are federally protected.

the pond. You could also access the pond from one of several large parking lots, which might be easier if you have little ones with you.

MILES AND DIRECTIONS

0.00 Begin at the Grassy Point trailhead.

0.20 Reach the northernmost point of the trail. Head south.

0.50 Come to an intersection; stay straight and at the next intersection (just up ahead), take a left to head toward Grassy Point.

0.75 Reach the end of Grassy Point, where you can sit on one of the benches or use the public viewing scope. Head back the way you came.

1.00 Meet an intersection and go right. At the next junction, turn left to head back toward the parking lot.

1.2 Arrive back at the trailhead.

The view of the beach from across the pond

7 FORT WETHERILL STATE PARK

There are numerous places to swim along the southern shores of Rhode Island—just take your pick of the dozens of sandy beaches that dot the shoreline. But instead of pushing through the crowds at the beaches, consider visiting the historic Fort Wetherill State Park. The crystal-clear waters and lack of tourists mean more room for you, and the potential to see some unique marine life.

Start: At the trailhead at the scuba lot and ruins parking lot
Elevation gain: 60 feet
Distance: 0.55 mile out and back
Difficulty: Easy
Hiking time: About 30 minutes
Fees and permits: Fee required
Trail contact: Fort Wetherill State Park, Fort Wetherill Rd., Jamestown, RI 02835; (401) 884-2010; https://riparks.ri.gov/parks/fort-wetherill-state-park
Dog-friendly: Allowed on leash

Trail surface: Pavement, dirt, and rocks
Land status: Rhode Island State Parks
Nearest town: Jamestown, RI
Other trail users: Cyclists and scuba divers
Temperature of water: 70°F
Body of water: Atlantic Ocean
Water availability: None
Maps: Fort Wetherill State Park map
Toilets: Yes, at the trailhead
Wheelchair compatibility: No
Family-friendly: Yes

FINDING THE TRAILHEAD

From Providence, take I-95 South for approximately 12 miles. Keep left at the fork to continue on RI-4 South, following signs for North Kingstown. After 10 miles of driving, continue onto US-1 South for 0.75 mile and use the right lane to take the ramp to RI-138 East toward Jamestown/Newport. Keep left to continue on RI-138 East for approximately 6 miles and then take the exit toward Jamestown. The ramp turns into Conanicus Avenue, which you'll travel on for 1.5 miles. The road takes a slight left, at which point it becomes Walcott Avenue. Drive approximately 0.5 mile and then turn left onto Fort Wetherill Road. End at the parking lot. Scuba lot GPS: N41 28.7628', W71 21.6216'; ruins lot GPS: N41 28.7088', W71 21.5082'

THE HIKE

There are many types of visitors who frequent Fort Wetherill State Park. Researchers love the area due to the abundant marine life that calls the coves home. During a recent visit, there were "Save the Bay" researchers doing some work in the coves, finding some seahorses and tropical fish in the waters. There are history buffs who like to walk the ruins around Battery Varnum to learn more about the stories of this area. Then there are adventurers who simply like to walk along the bluffs to see the jagged rocks that keep the ocean at bay. This is also a very popular scuba spot, where many divers come to train for bigger dives in bigger waters.

But if you're reading this book, you're likely one of the people who like to visit this place for the warm, crystal-clear water to swim in. First, hop on the trail between the two coves that starts on the southern end of the scuba parking lot. The trail cuts through the trees and spits you out onto two observation points. You can see for miles on a clear day.

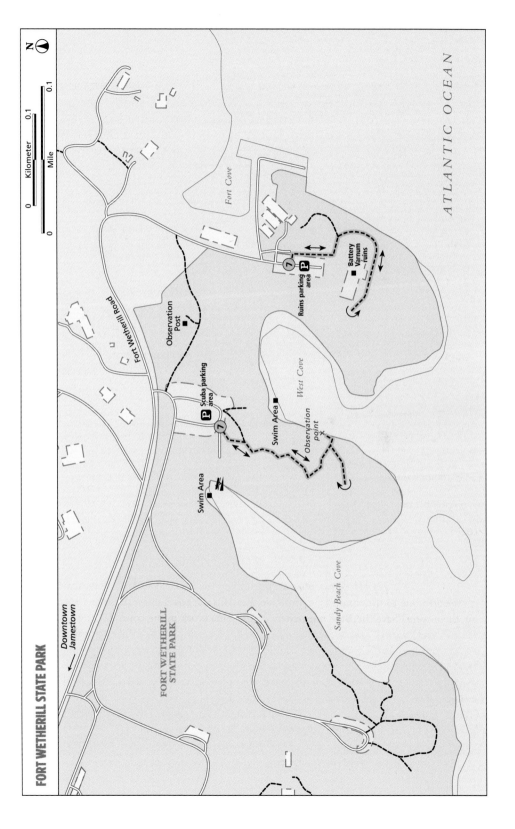

FORT WETHERILL STATE PARK

N

← Downtown Jamestown

Fort Wetherill Road

FORT WETHERILL STATE PARK

Observation Post ■

Scuba parking area P 7

Swim Area ■

Swim Area ■

Observation point ✕

West Cove

Sandy Beach Cove

Fort Cove

Ruins parking area P 7

Battery Varnum ruins ■

ATLANTIC OCEAN

Kilometer 0 0.1 0.1
Mile 0 0.1

Crystal clear water as far as the eye can see at one of the beaches HOLLY CURTIS

Head back the way you came to return to the parking lot.

When you get back to the car, grab your swimming gear and head down to one of the two coves that flank either side of the peninsula you just walked on. The West Cove is to your left when facing the water, while on the right sits Sandy Beach Cove. Sandy Beach Cove has, you guessed it, a sandy beach and bottom, so it's nice on your feet if you don't have water shoes. Did I mention that the water is crystal clear and you can see all the marine life that swims below the surface? West Cove, where folks can be seen fishing and sunbathing, has large rocks that flank the sides.

When you've had your fill of swimming, get back in your car to head to the ruins parking lot, just east on Fort Wetherill Road. Here you can do a second hike to Battery Varnum, which was used back in the World War II era. It was the largest fort of the Coast Defenses of Narragansett Bay at the time. It was decommissioned and acquired by the State of Rhode Island to use as a state park in the 1970s.

Looking back at the coves in the park
HOLLY CURTIS

The hike is short and brings you south out of the parking lot heading toward the ruins. You'll round the eastern side of them and see what's left of the old battery. There is lots of graffiti there now, but it gives it an artistic look. Don't forget to turn around and check out the views too! Then return the way you came.

MILES AND DIRECTIONS

Hike from the scuba lot:

- 0.00 Begin at the southern end of the scuba lot. Head south on the trail.
- 0.10 Head left to check out the observation area. Get back to the main trail and veer left to check out another observation area.

A MECCA FOR SCUBA DIVERS
There is so much to do at Fort Wetherill State Park, including swimming, boating, and checking out the fort ruins (don't miss out on those!). But Fort Wetherill is also home to some of the best scuba diving sites in the region. Divers from all over make the trek to Fort Wetherill to partake in the clear waters and the abundant marine life. There are several dive sites within the park, so be on the lookout for scuba divers surfacing after their adventure!

0.15 Reach the end of the trail and an observation area. Turn around and return to the parking area.

0.30 Arrive back at the scuba lot. Swim in one of the two coves here and then get in your car to drive to the hike around the ruins.

Hike from the ruins lot:

0.00 Start at the ruins parking lot, on the eastern side. Turn right to head toward Battery Varnum.

0.05 Turn left to make your way around the ruins, coming at them from their eastern side.

0.15 Reach the end of the ruins. Turn around and head back to your car.

0.20 Turn right to continue to the parking lot.

0.25 Arrive back at the ruins parking lot.

A perfect place to wade in the water and observe marine life HOLLY CURTIS

8 PECK POND

While everyone else hits the beaches of Rhode Island the minute temperatures rise, I head north to get some peace and quiet. Despite its modest size, the 100-acre Casimir Pulaski Memorial State Park is packed full of things to see. You can choose to spend all day swimming in the pond; the beach is ideal for sunbathing in between dips. But if you need to break things up, you can also hike around the pond as well as try your hand at some trout fishing.

Start: At the Blue Dot trailhead
Elevation gain: 200 feet
Distance: 3.2-mile lollipop
Difficulty: Easy
Hiking time: About 1.5 hours
Fees and permits: No fee required
Trail contact: Casimir Pulaski Memorial State Park and Recreational Area, 151 Pulaski Rd., Chepachet, RI 02814; (401) 723-7892; https://riparks.ri.gov/parks/pulaski-state-park
Dog-friendly: Allowed on leash on trails; prohibited on the beach

Trail surface: Dirt and rock
Land status: George Washington Management Area
Nearest town: Putnam, CT
Other trail users: None in summer
Temperature of water: 75°F
Body of water: Peck Pond
Water availability: At the changing rooms
Maps: Pulaski State Park trail map
Toilets: Yes
Wheelchair compatibility: No
Family-friendly: Yes, with supervision

FINDING THE TRAILHEAD

From Providence, take US-6 West for almost 12 miles. Continue straight onto RI-101 West (do not veer left to stay on US-6). Stay on RI-101 for 8 miles. Turn right onto RI-94 North for 5.6 miles and then turn left onto US-44 West. After 1 mile, turn right onto Pulaski Road and into the state park. Find your way to the main parking area for beach access. GPS: N41 55.9062', W71 47.8254'

THE HIKE

This undiscovered gem in northern Rhode Island gives visitors the joy of heading out of the city and into the wilderness without the crowds of the beaches. It sits right at the border with Connecticut but is still within an hour of Providence.

If you're doing the hike prior to hitting up the beach at the pond's edge, start to the east of the parking lot. The lot can fill quickly on hot weekends, so come early or on a weekday if you want more seclusion on the beach. Although it might get crowded, the trails are surprisingly quiet, since most folks come here for the beach. The hike starts along the Blue Dot Trail, which is easily identified by a white blaze with a blue dot in the middle of it.

You'll pass the White Blaze Trail on your right, but continue straight and then immediately take the right fork to get off the Blue Dot Trail. You'll be veering away from Peck Pond at this point. Unfortunately, the trails here don't have that many blazes, so it might be a bit confusing because the next few forks occur one on top of the other. In the course of 0.2 mile, you'll stay right at a fork and then left until you finally hit a T-intersection.

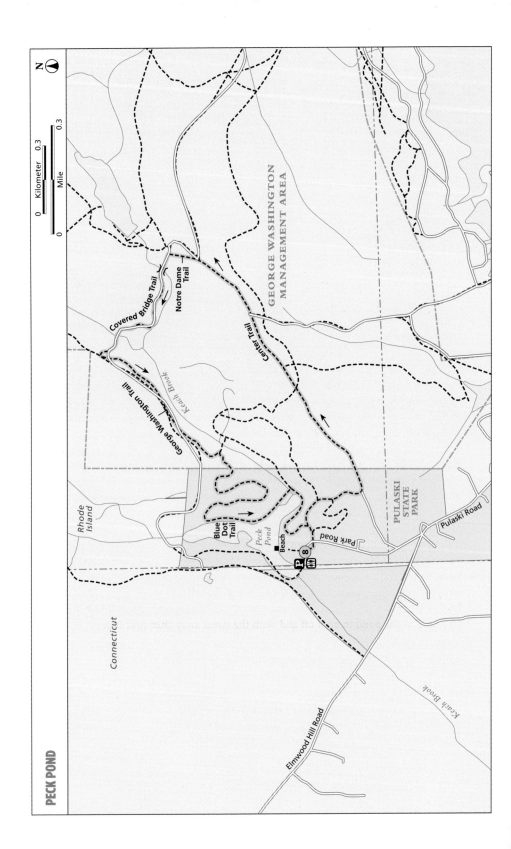

PECK POND

George Washington Trail
Covered Bridge Trail
Notre Dame Trail
Carter Trail
George Washington Trail
Keach Brook
Rhode Island
Connecticut
Blue Dot Trail
Peck Pond
Beach
Park Road
Pulaski Road
Elmwood Hill Road
Keach Brook
GEORGE WASHINGTON MANAGEMENT AREA
PULASKI STATE PARK

N

0   Kilometer   0.3
0   Mile   0.3

The trail at Casimir Pulaski State Park

If you go right, it'll bring you back to the park road; instead, take a left to head northeast along Center Trail. There are various trails on your left and right, but just continue straight until you reach a gate. Go through it if it's open or around if it's not. Take the trail all the way to your left (there are three trails) and head toward the covered bridge.

Turn left to go through the covered bridge. As you walk along the Covered Bridge Trail (green blazes), you'll pass through wetlands and swamps, so the trail may be wet or muddy in places. Remember to walk right through the mud to minimize trail erosion.

When you reach another T-intersection, take a left onto the George Washington Trail, indicated by orange blazes. The wetlands and swamps will be to your left as you walk southwest to get back to the trailhead. Hemlocks line this trail, and you'll find plenty of pinecones on the ground.

Eventually, after about 0.5 mile, the trail will veer left, and then you'll take the trail on your right to get back on the Blue Dot Trail. This trail is filled with lots of roots and wet spots as you near Peck Pond. Be on the lookout for beavers as you get closer. You'll likely see a lot of beaver evidence among the trees that line the pond. The Blue Dot Trail will bring you all the way back to your car, where you can then grab your beach accessories and head to the pond to cool off and wash the sweat away after your hike.

MILES AND DIRECTIONS

0.00   Start on the east side of the parking lot at the Blue Dot trailhead.

0.02   The White Blaze Trail veers to the right; stay straight.

0.04   At the fork in the trail, take the right fork to get off the Blue Dot Trail.

0.10   Stay right at the fork.

0.20   Stay left at the next fork.

0.30   At the T-intersection, take a left onto Center Trail.

A picnic shelter next to the beach with great views of the pond

1.10   Take the left fork to get on Notre Dame Trail.

1.20   Take a left onto the Covered Bridge Trail, which follows green blazes.

1.30   Go through the covered bridge.

1.60   Take a left onto the George Washington Trail, which follows orange blazes.

2.10   Take a right back onto the Blue Dot Trail.

2.90   Take a right to stay on the Blue Dot Trail.

3.20   Arrive back at the trailhead.

THE DIFFERENCE BETWEEN HARDWOOD AND SOFTWOOD TREES?

Most people can look at a tree and tell if it has pine needles or leaves or something in between. But there are scientific terms for these things, too. Hardwood trees, also known as angiosperms, have seeds with a protective covering (think acorns, nuts, etc.) and commonly have leafy leaves (rather than needle-like). Hardwood trees include maple, oak, ash, elm, and more. Most hardwood trees go dormant in the winter, meaning they drop their leaves, which is why they are also often called deciduous trees.

Softwood trees, also known as gymnosperms, do not have seeds but rather pinecones, and usually possess needlelike "leaves." Typically, softwood trees are of the pine, cedar, hemlock, and spruce variety. These are trees that don't usually go dormant in the winter and retain their needles all year—also known as non-deciduous. But deciduous does not always equal hardwood and non-deciduous does not always equal softwood.

Generally speaking, the wood of hardwood trees is actually harder (hence the name) than softwoods, but not always. The strongest wood in the world is Australian buloke, which is a hardwood. The other top four strongest woods also happen to be hardwoods. However, the softest wood in the world is balsa wood, which is also a hardwood!

MASSACHUSETTS

A swimming spot hidden from the tourists visiting Cape Cod

9 WELLFLEET KETTLE PONDS

Cape Cod has no shortage of pristine, sandy beaches that stretch for miles. Unfortunately, it also has no shortage of tourists and crowded shores. Instead of opting for a day at the beach, head inland to one of the many kettle ponds scattered throughout the small town of Wellfleet. Strap on your hiking shoes, grab your towel, and head out into the sandy forests of Cape Cod to experience a secret treasure.

Start: At the Long Pond parking area
Elevation gain: 170 feet
Distance: 1.9 miles out and back
Difficulty: Easy
Hiking time: About 1 hour
Fees and permits: Fee/beach sticker required
Trail contact: Cape Cod National Seashore, 99 Marconi Site Rd., Wellfleet, MA 02667; (508) 255-3421; www.nps.gov/caco
Dog-friendly: Not allowed
Trail surface: Gravel and dirt
Land status: National Park Service

Nearest town: Wellfleet, MA
Other trail users: Mountain bikers
Body of water: Long Pond, Gull Pond, and Spectacle Pond
Temperature of water: 75°F
Water availability: None
Maps: Cape Cod National Seashore map
Toilets: Yes, at Long and Gull Ponds
Wheelchair compatibility: At Long and Gull Ponds
Family-friendly: Yes, at Long and Gull Ponds

FINDING THE TRAILHEAD

From Boston, take I-93 South for 10 miles, then use the left 2 lanes to take exit 7 for MA-3 South toward Cape Cod. Continue on MA-3 South for approximately 43 miles and then merge onto US-6 East for about 36 miles. At the traffic circle, take the second exit to stay on US-6 East for an additional 11 miles. Turn left onto Main Street, and after 0.25 mile turn right onto Long Pond Road. The parking area is about 1 mile down the road on the left, across from Long Pond beach. GPS: N41 56.7348', W70 0.6174'

Finding Gull Pond: From the Long Pond parking lot, head west on Long Pond Road. After 0.7 mile, turn right onto Lawrence Road, then turn right again onto US-6 East. Drive another 0.5 mile and turn right onto Gull Pond Road. Travel for 1.1 miles and turn left onto School House Hill Road. At the fork, stay right to head to the parking lot at Gull Pond. There is enough parking for 30 or so vehicles. GPS: N41 57.36084', W70 0.80298'

THE HIKE

Before you start the hike, make sure you pop by Wellfleet's sticker office, located on Wellfleet Pier, to grab your parking sticker (if you don't, your car will be towed at your expense). Once you've parked at the Long Pond beach lot, make your way left onto Long Pond Road. After just a few hundred feet, take the dirt road on your left.

The dirt road is for off-road vehicles and mountain bikes, but hikers also use this area. There are no blazes or signs here other than a few on trees that say "private property." Please stick to the road and do not trespass into the woods. There will be several trails that intersect the road you're walking on—these are mountain bike trails. Be cautious around these areas, as mountain bikers can come up on you quickly.

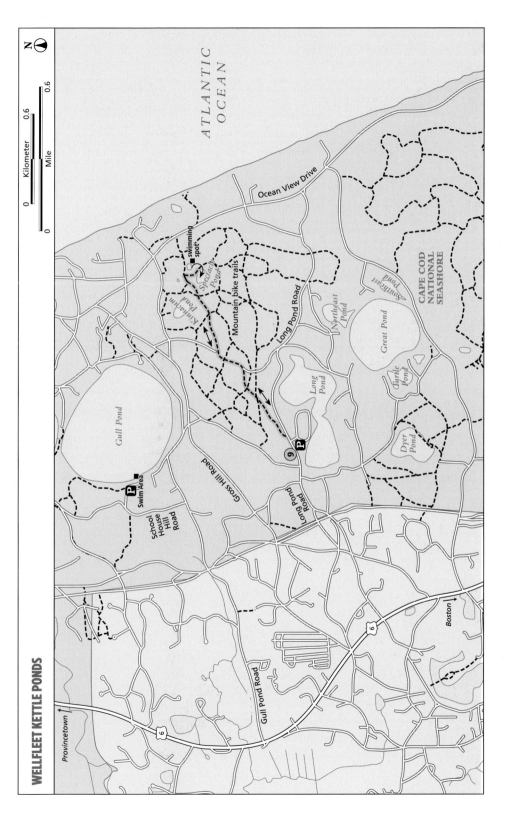

WELLFLEET KETTLE PONDS

N

0   Kilometer   0.6

0   Mile   0.6

ATLANTIC OCEAN

Ocean View Drive

swimming spot

Spectacle Pond

Kinnacum Pond

Mountain bike trails

Long Pond Road

Northeast Pond

Southeast Pond

CAPE COD NATIONAL SEASHORE

Great Pond

Turtle Pond

Long Pond

Dyer Pond

Gull Pond

School House Hill Road

Swim Area

P

Gross Hill Road

Long Pond Road

6

P

6

Gull Pond Road

Boston

6

Provincetown

Gull Pond is much more popular and
easier to get to but just as spectacular

For seclusion, head to Spectacle Pond—tourists don't know about this place

Although there are no blazes or signs, the trail is easy to follow because it's the only one that is wide enough for a car to travel on. Go straight on the wide path; around the 0.4-mile mark, you'll merge with another road and continue straight. Another 0.1 mile brings you to another fork, where you'll veer right. Keep heading straight on the wide path. Eventually you'll reach a small parking lot (for ATVers) and signs indicating that you've made it to Spectacle Pond.

Take a right when you get to the parking lot and hike the small trail to the entrance to Spectacle Pond. There is a small dock with a few stairs leading into the water. Head on in for a swim until you're ready to continue your journey.

The next leg will bring you back the way you came to return to your car. Again, simply follow the widest path the entire way. When the road forks, stick to the right to head back to the Long Pond parking lot. Once back at the lot, feel free to swim in Long Pond, which is just across the road from the parking area. Or you can drive up to Gull Pond (see directions above). This is the largest of the three kettle ponds and is often used by anglers. There is a small beach at its shore that you can sunbathe on and watch the ospreys catch their prey in the water.

WHAT IS A KETTLE POND?

Kettle ponds are glacially formed basins that were carved out about 18,000 years ago when the large ice sheet that covered half of North America began to retreat. The ice sheet broke off and left chunks of ice that formed large holes in the earth and created these clear, naturally acidic freshwater pools. These ponds are extremely important habitat for many types of plant and animal species, so it's important to take special care when entering these waters. Always use the restroom prior to going in; remove all sunscreens, soaps, bug sprays, and so on from your body; and carry out all trash.

The trails to the more remote kettle ponds are ATV roads that are impassable for most vehicles

MILES AND DIRECTIONS

0.00 Start at the Long Pond parking lot. Head left (northeast) on Long Pond Road.

0.05 Take a left onto the dirt road.

0.40 Merge with another road but keep straight.

0.50 Veer right at the fork.

0.95 Take a right onto a small trail toward Spectacle Pond. Swim and then head back the way you came.

1.40 Veer left to continue on the wide, dirt road.

1.50 Veer right to continue on the dirt road.

1.85 Take a right onto Long Pond Road.

1.90 Arrive back at the Long Pond parking lot.

10 MYSTIC LAKES STATE PARK

Escape the city and unwind in beautiful Mystic Lakes State Park. The Mystic River is one of Massachusetts's best-protected streams, which means swimming in the lakes offers a pristine experience. The lakes are filled with abundant wildlife and recreationists. After a brisk hike along both Upper and Lower Mystic Lakes, take a dip from Shannon Beach in the northeast corner of Upper Mystic Lake.

Start: At the Mystic Lakes State Park parking area on the east side of the lakes
Elevation gain: 25 feet
Distance: 2.6 miles out and back
Difficulty: Easy
Hiking time: About 1.5 hours
Fees and permits: No fee required
Trail contact: Mystic Lakes State Park, 481 Mystic Valley Pkwy., Medford, MA 02155; (857) 702-3884; www.mass.gov/locations/mystic -lakes-state-park
Dog-friendly: Allowed on leash on trails; prohibited on the beach

Trail surface: Pavement and sand
Land status: Massachusetts Department of Conservation & Recreation
Nearest town: Medford, MA
Other trail users: Cyclists
Body of water: Upper Mystic Lake
Temperature of water: 70°F
Water availability: None
Maps: Mystic Lakes State Park map
Toilets: Yes, at the bathhouse
Wheelchair compatibility: Some of the trail is on pavement.
Family-friendly: Yes

FINDING THE TRAILHEAD

From Boston, take I-93 North for approximately 4 miles. Take exit 22 to merge onto MA-16 West/Mystic Valley Parkway toward Arlington. After about 1.5 miles, turn right onto Winthrop Street; at the traffic circle, take the fourth exit onto High Street. Travel for approximately 1.3 miles and at the next traffic circle, take the first exit onto Mystic Valley Parkway. Parking will be on your left at the northern end of Lower Mystic Lake. GPS: N42 26.466', W71 8.6676'

THE HIKE

This quiet haven on the outskirts of Boston is a perfect place for those wanting to escape the hustle and bustle and take a walk along a beautiful part of the Mystic River. If you don't own a car, not to worry—this area can be accessed by public transportation (take the Green Line to the 80 bus to Arlington Center, then it's a short walk from there).

The only place you can swim at Mystic Lakes State Park is at Shannon Beach. It's a small, sandy area on the northeastern tip of Upper Mystic Lake. There is a brand-new bathhouse for visitors to use at their leisure, along with plenty of other amenities, like a playground for little kids. I suggest going on the hike first and then ending your day at Shannon Beach.

The hike starts on the eastern side of Shannon Beach on the paved path. Folks in wheelchairs and families with strollers will appreciate this hike, as it's on pavement and then packed-down dirt. The trail skirts the eastern banks of both Upper and Lower Mystic Lakes, where you can view wildlife and those recreating out on the water. Motorized

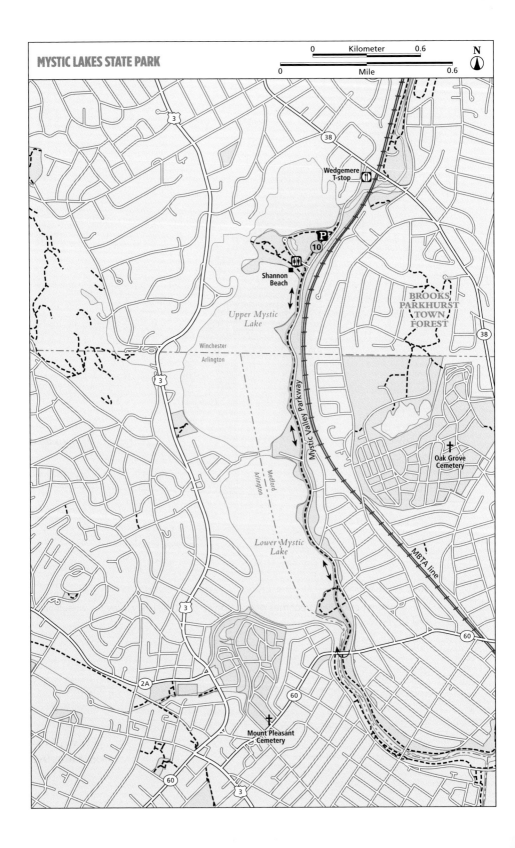

MYSTIC LAKES STATE PARK

0 Kilometer 0.6

0 Mile 0.6

N

38

Wedgemere
T-stop

P
10

Shannon
Beach

*Upper Mystic
Lake*

Winchester
Arlington

BROOKS
PARKHURST
TOWN
FOREST

38

Mystic Valley Parkway

Oak Grove
Cemetery

*Medford
Arlington*

*Lower Mystic
Lake*

MBTA line

3

60

2A

60

Mount Pleasant
Cemetery

60

3

boats are allowed in Lower Mystic Lake, but only nonmotorized watercraft are permitted in Upper Mystic Lake.

You'll continue south the entire way until you reach the southern tip of Lower Mystic Lake. There is a spot close to the water at the end here, but heed the sign that says "No Swimming" and refrain from jumping in. Instead, head back the way you came to Shannon Beach so you can jump in the water.

MILES AND DIRECTIONS

0.00 Start at the paved sidewalk next to Shannon Beach and walk south.

0.40 The pavement ends and becomes packed-down dirt (still likely okay for wheelchairs and strollers).

0.80 Cross over the road that heads down to the Medford Boat Club. Continue south.

1.30 Reach the southern tip of Lower Mystic Lake. Turn around and head back the way you came.

1.80 Cross over the road that heads down to the Medford Boat Club. Continue north.

2.20 The trail becomes pavement again.

2.60 Arrive back at Shannon Beach.

11 CHAPEL FALLS

The 173 acres of Chapel Brook Reservation were given as a gift from Mrs. Henry T. Curtis to remember her husband, who passed earlier. The reservation includes the 1,420-foot-high summit of Pony Mountain, which overlooks the Berkshire Mountains to the south. But it also includes an incredibly serene swimming hole at the base of Chapel Falls—a series of three drops totaling 45 feet.

Start: At the Chapel Falls trailhead
Elevation gain: 130 feet
Distance: 0.5 mile out and back
Difficulty: Easy
Hiking time: About 30 minutes
Fees and permits: No fee required
Trail contact: The Trustees of Reservations—Chapel Brook Reservation, 200 High St., Boston, MA 02110; (978) 921-1944; https://thetrustees.org/place/chapel-brook
Dog-friendly: Allowed on leash

Trail surface: Dirt and rocks/roots
Land status: The Trustees
Nearest town: Ashfield, MA
Other trail users: Hunters
Body of water: Chapel Brook
Temperature of water: 65°F
Water availability: None
Maps: Chapel Brook Trail map
Toilets: No
Wheelchair compatibility: No
Family-friendly: No

FINDING THE TRAILHEAD

From Springfield, take I-91 North for approximately 17 miles. Take exit 25 for MA-9 toward Hadley/Amherst. At the traffic circle, take the second exit onto Damon Road. Drive for just over 1 mile and continue onto Bridge Road for an additional 2.3 miles. At the next traffic circle, take the first exit onto North Main Street. After 0.5 mile, veer right onto MA-9 West/Haydenville Road. Continue on this road for approximately 4 miles. Turn right onto North Street, which then turns into Ashfield Road/Ashfield Williamsburg Valley Road. Stay on this road for approximately 6.5 miles. Parking is on the right-hand side before the bridge and the left-hand side after the bridge. There are enough parking spots for around 12 cars. GPS: N42 28.9194', W72 45.6216'

THE HIKE

You can park on the southeastern or northwestern side of Chapel Brook along Williamsburg Road. If you park in the northwestern lot, do not take the trail at this parking lot, as it will bring you up the Summit Trail to Chapel Ledge (although this is a nice hike). Instead, walk south on Williamsburg Road to the other parking lot across the road and start on the Two Bridges Trail.

Chapel Falls can be heard from the parking lot and is just a few hundred feet from the start of the trail. Head down and you'll see the first of three drops, which is a 10-foot fan waterfall (see the sidebar in the Enders Falls chapter to get the lowdown on the different types of waterfalls). The next set falls off the edge at a much lower gradient and is considered a slide waterfall. The final and most dramatic of the falls is the third one. It drops a total of 20 feet from the edge and onto a 5-foot slide waterfall.

All the pools at the bottom of each of the falls are great options to take a plunge. The pool at the third set of falls has a bit of debris around the edges, likely due to all the trail work being done. Just use caution here.

CHAPEL FALLS

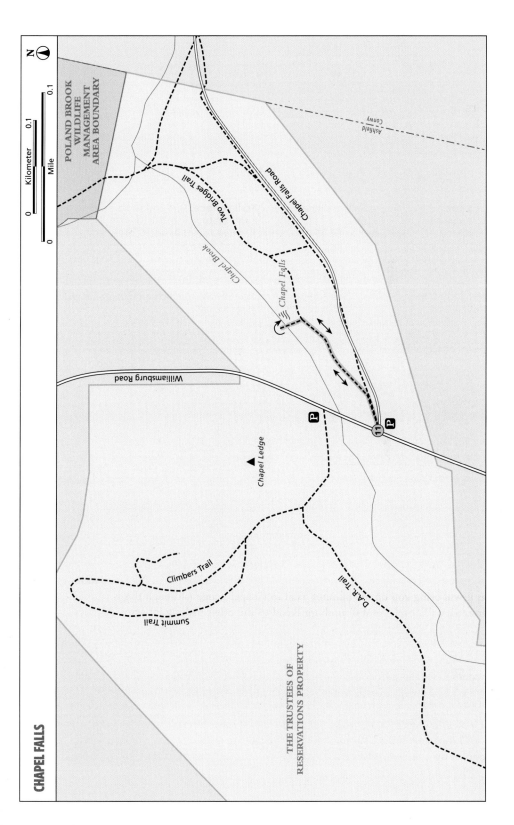

N

Kilometer   0.1

0

Mile   0.1

0

POLAND BROOK
WILDLIFE
MANAGEMENT
AREA BOUNDARY

Two Bridges Trail

Chapel Brook

Chapel Falls Road

Chapel Falls

Williamsburg Road

Ashfield
Conwy

P

P

Chapel Ledge

Climbers Trail

Summit Trail

D.A.R. Trail

THE TRUSTEES OF
RESERVATIONS PROPERTY

The trail is undergoing some repairs due to the heavy traffic, and several sections are roped off because of the fragile ecosystem and too many visitors going off-trail. Make sure to stay on the marked trails and only enter the pools where it is allowed to do so. Do not attempt to stomp over the revegetation efforts.

For a bigger adventure, head back to the parking lot and hike up the Summit Trail on the other side of the road. This will bring you up Pony Mountain and Chapel Ledge—a 100-foot rock face looking south into the Berkshire Mountains.

The first swimming hole at Chapel Falls

Looking downstream at the first swimming hole at Chapel Falls

MILES AND DIRECTIONS

0.00 Start at the southeastern parking lot at the Two Bridges Trail. Take a left to head down to the river's edge.

0.10 First set of waterfalls.

0.25 Reach the second and third sets of waterfalls. Go back the way you came.

0.50 Arrive back at the trailhead.

12 **WHIRLEY BATHS**

Although called Whirley Baths, the temperature of the water is not that of bathwater. There's a reason it's called the Cold River, and it isn't because of its personality. Temperatures in the Cold River can get as low as 55°F, so be careful dipping into the river. The coldness of the water might be welcome, though, on hot days. The area is blanketed with small holes that are a bit like private Jacuzzis—just without 100-degree water.

Start: Off the MA-2 pullout near Mohawk Trail State Forest
Elevation gain: 30 feet
Distance: 1.0 mile out and back (if parking in the preferred parking area)
Difficulty: Easy
Hiking time: About 30 minutes
Fees and permits: No fee required
Trail contact: Mohawk Trail State Forest, Cold River Rd., Charlemont, MA 01339; (413) 339-5504; www.mass.gov/locations/mohawk-trail-state-forest
Dog-friendly: Allowed on leash
Trail surface: Pavement, dirt, and rocks/roots

Land status: Massachusetts Department of Conservation & Recreation
Nearest town: Charlemont, MA
Other trail users: None
Body of water: Cold River
Temperature of water: 65°F
Water availability: None
Maps: Mohawk Trail State Forest map
Toilets: No
Wheelchair compatibility: No
Family-friendly: Yes (although this area is known to have nude swimming)

FINDING THE TRAILHEAD

From Springfield, take I-91 North for approximately 35 miles. Take exit 43 for MA-2 West/MA-2A East toward Greenfield Center/North Adams. At the traffic circle, take the third exit onto MA-2 West and continue on this road for approximately 21 miles. You'll see the pullout right at Whirley Baths, but signs say "Live Parking Only." If you choose to park here, know that it is only 30-minute parking and is strictly enforced by local officials. If you want to spend more time here, keep traveling down MA-2 until you reach a large pullout on the right-hand side, just before the bridge going toward Mohawk Trail State Forest. Then walk the road back to Whirley Baths. This is an extremely busy road, so please use caution when walking on the road. GPS: N42 38.1504', W72 56.088'

THE HIKE

The road to get to Whirley Baths brings you through some of the most scenic spots in all of Massachusetts. Because of that, it's also one of the most popular areas to go for a scenic drive. After parking just south of the Mohawk Trail State Forest sign in the large gravel parking lot, head south on MA-2. If you have little kids with you, keep them close and away from the roadside to prevent accidents. It can't be emphasized enough how busy this road is. Better yet, drop your kids off along with an adult at the "Live Parking Only" pullout and then park your car farther up the road. That way your little ones won't have to walk at all on the busy road.

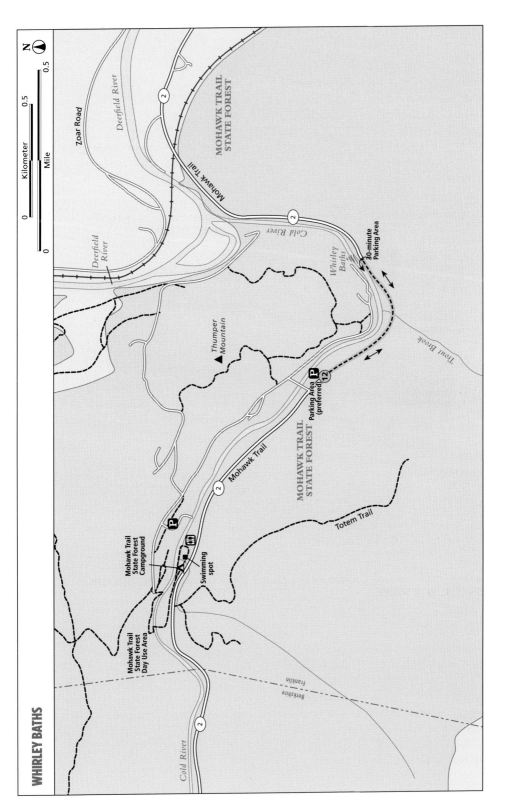

WHIRLEY BATHS

N

Kilometer
0   0.5   0.5

Mile
0   0.5

Zoar Road

Deerfield River

Deerfield River

MOHAWK TRAIL
STATE FOREST

Mohawk Trail

2

2

Cold River

Mohawk Trail

Whirley Baths

20-minute
Parking Area

Trout Brook

▲ *Thumper Mountain*

2

Mohawk Trail

P
(12)
Parking Area
(preferred)

MOHAWK TRAIL
STATE FOREST

Totem Trail

P

Mohawk Trail
State Forest
Campground

Swimming
spot

Mohawk Trail
State Forest
Day Use Area

Cold River

2

Berkshire
Franklin

There are no official trails to Whirley Baths; use the ones already established by other visitors

After about 0.5 mile of walking, you'll reach the pullout that says "Live Parking Only" and a small trail that goes down to the river. There has been some damage due to Hurricane Irene back in 2011, so be careful as you make your way there. Enjoy the cascades and the small pools found throughout this section of the Cold River. Contrary to what many visitors have said, Whirley Baths is not in the Deerfield River but rather a tributary of it.

THE HISTORY OF THE MOHAWK TRAIL

Before European settlement, the land around this area in Massachusetts was used by the Mohawk tribe (as well as some smaller tribes). These areas were lush in salmon and other fish that the Mohawk used to trade for other goods. The Mohawk Trail was used as a means to head to trading areas as well as travel in general.

Later, the trail was used by the French and their Native American allies during the French and Indian War. It was also used by the Mohawk to fight against King Philip, who was the leader of the Wampanoag Confederacy at the time. And the famed traitor Benedict Arnold used this same route for recruitment purposes during the American Revolution.

The road then became more modern and provided the link between western Massachusetts and the rest of the Commonwealth. It is now a scenic byway that thousands travel every year. It is also home to some of the oldest forests in the state, with white pines that tower over 140 feet.

There is also another swimming hole at the Mohawk Trail State Forest Day Use Area. When you get back to your car, drive northwest on MA-2 for about 0.8 mile, where you'll see the state forest entrance on your right. Park in an available parking spot and head down to the water; the swimming hole can easily be seen. This is likely the better option for those not wanting to risk getting their cars towed or walking along MA-2 for an extended period of time. The pool at the day-use area does not have any cascades or natural waterslides like Whirley Baths but is a great alternative if needed.

MILES AND DIRECTIONS

0.00 Start at the parking lot off MA-2 near the Mohawk Trail State Forest bridge. Head south.

0.50 Take a left to head down the small trail to the river and Whirley Baths. When you're done in the water, head back the way you came.

1.00 Arrive back at the parking lot off MA-2.

One of several places to wade and swim

13 BELLEVUE FALLS

Some of the most beautiful swimming holes are in the most unassuming places. Bellevue Falls is no exception. The falls are located just off to the side of Bellevue Cemetery. But don't worry about walking over headstones or potentially waking any ghosts along the way. The parking lot and waterfalls don't cross any of the graves. This gem of a swimming hole is great no matter your age. The water stays a cool 70°F thanks to the shaded banks that are plentiful with trees.

Start: At the small parking area near the southwestern border of Bellevue Cemetery
Elevation gain: 45 feet
Distance: 0.1 mile out and back
Difficulty: Easy
Hiking time: About 30 minutes
Fees and permits: No fee required
Trail contact: City of Lawrence, 200 Common St., Lawrence, MA 01840; (978) 620-3000; www.cityoflawrence.com/155/Bellevue-Cemetery

Dog-friendly: Not allowed
Trail surface: Pavement, dirt, and rocks/roots
Land status: City of Lawrence
Nearest town: Lawrence, MA
Other trail users: None
Body of water: Dry Brook
Temperature of water: 70°F
Water availability: None
Maps: Bellevue Cemetery map
Toilets: No
Wheelchair compatibility: No
Family-friendly: Yes

FINDING THE TRAILHEAD

From Springfield, take I-91 North for approximately 17 miles. Take exit 25 for MA-9 toward Hadley/Amherst. At the traffic circle, take the second exit onto Damon Road and continue for 1 mile, where it turns into Bridge Road. After 2 miles, take the first exit at the traffic circle onto North Main Street and continue onto MA-9 West for approximately 12 miles. Turn right onto Shaw Road/Willcutt Road/Cummington Road for approximately 3 miles. Turn left onto MA-116 North for 17 miles. Take a slight left onto Leonard Street and then turn left after 0.5 mile onto Bellevue Avenue. After 0.2 mile, you'll enter Bellevue Cemetery.

Please be kind and respectful to anyone who is visiting the cemetery. Follow the western edge of the cemetery by taking as many right turns as possible. You'll only travel for about 0.2 mile to reach a very small parking turnout on the right-hand side of the road. You're there when you see a short section of white fence. GPS: N42 36.141', W73 7.5258'

THE HIKE

There are no signs indicating that there are waterfalls in this cemetery or near the parking lot. The trail to head down to Bellevue Falls is an obvious dirt path between the trees at the parking lot. The well-traveled footpath is easy to follow, and within a few minutes you reach the falls as you descend to the brook.

The waterfall is only about 6 feet high and is split by a large rock in the middle. This is a popular spot among younger folks, who enjoy all areas around the falls. There are large boulders and ledges that are great for sunbathing on both sides of the pool. A little bit upstream of the falls, the stream is shallower and safer for children to wade.

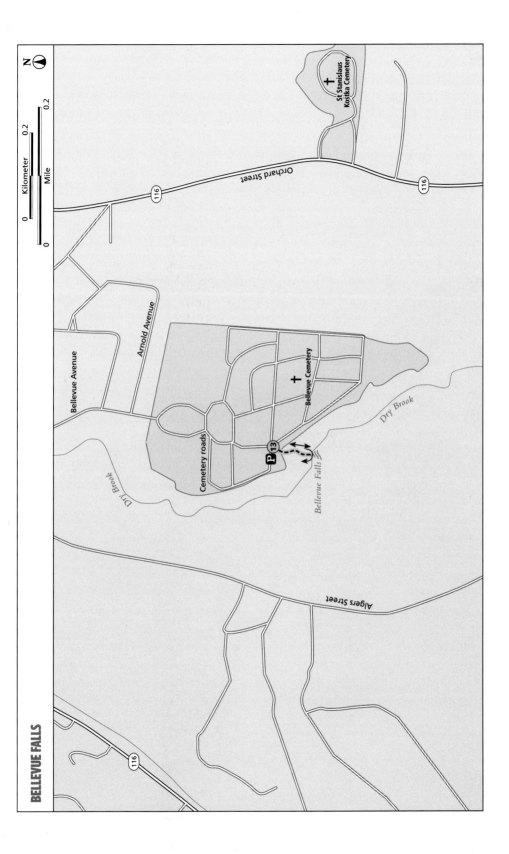

N

Kilometer
0   0.2   0.2

Mile
0   0.2

116

Orchard Street

St Stanislaus
Kostka Cemetery

Bellevue Avenue

Arnold Avenue

Dry Brook

Cemetery roads

Bellevue Cemetery

P 13

Bellevue Falls

Dry Brook

116

Algers Street

116

The trail to the river is surrounded by a young forest

The pool at the base of the falls

As far as swimming holes go, this is likely one of the best in Massachusetts. The waterfall isn't particularly spectacular, but the pool is the real hero here. The large pool allows for dozens of people to comfortably wade and swim without getting in each other's way. You can even jump in from the ledges on the side since the bottom is easily seen through the crystal-clear water.

Due to the ease of access, popularity, and lack of regular maintenance at this swimming hole, there tends to be a bit more trash than at the other swimming holes on this list. Bring a reusable trash bag when you visit Bellevue Falls to help pick up what others might have left behind. There are no garbage cans or other facilities on the property, so make sure to pack out what you pack in (and pick up!). Hopefully, with minimal effort from all visitors, this place will be available to enjoy for years to come.

MILES AND DIRECTIONS

0.00 Start at the parking lot on the southwestern side of the cemetery. Take the small trail in front of the parking lot and head toward the water.

0.05 Reach the falls. When you're done enjoying the water, turn around and head back the way you came.

0.10 Arrive back at your car in the small parking lot.

14 BENEDICT POND

A bit more off-the-beaten path resides this small pond in southwestern Massachusetts. Benedict Pond is a 35-acre man-made lake and one that shouldn't be disregarded just because of its size. This area has multiple trails that meet up with the loop that goes around the pond, including the Appalachian Trail. Get a view from every angle as you make your way around this loop!

Start: At the Benedict Pond Loop trailhead
Elevation gain: 115 feet
Distance: 1.7-mile loop
Difficulty: Easy
Hiking time: About 1 hour
Fees and permits: Fee required
Trail contact: Beartown State Forest, 69 Blue Hill Rd., Monterey, MA 01245; (413) 528-0904
Dog-friendly: Allowed on leash on trails; prohibited on the beach
Trail surface: Sand, dirt, and rocks/roots

Land status: Massachusetts Department of Conservation & Recreation
Nearest town: Monterey, MA
Other trail users: Horseback riders and mountain bikers
Body of water: Benedict Pond
Temperature of water: 75°F
Water availability: None
Maps: Benedict Pond Loop map
Toilets: Yes, at the bathhouse
Wheelchair compatibility: No
Family-friendly: Yes

FINDING THE TRAILHEAD

From Springfield, take I-90 West/Albany for approximately 35 miles. Take exit 10 for US-20 East and use the right lane to turn left and then immediately right onto MA-102 West. Travel for 4.6 miles and turn left onto US-7 South/South Street. Drive for 2.7 miles, then turn left onto Monument Valley Road. After 2 miles, you'll take a slight left onto Stony Brook Road for another 1.5 miles. It turns into Blue Hill Road; continue for another 1.4 miles. Turn left onto Benedict Pond Road and end at the parking lot. GPS: N42 12.1668', W73 17.3268'

THE HIKE

After European settlement, the area around Benedict Pond was owned by dairy farmer Fred Benedict in the late 1800s through the early 1900s. This is where the pond gets its name. Start the trail following the blue blazes to the right of the parking lot (the pond will be on your left as you walk). Download a trail map on your phone beforehand, as this trail has interpretive signs corresponding to the map.

The trail keeps close to the water's edge for the majority of the loop and rewards visitors with beautiful views of the pond. If you visit during June, the water's edge will have a snow-covered appearance due to the mountain laurel blooming. The flowers are fragrant and likely abuzz with pollinators.

Continue on the Blue Blaze Trail until you round the southeastern side of the pond and meet up with the Appalachian Trail. If you're visiting in August, you might encounter some thru-hikers along your hike. Some like to chat with visitors while others keep to themselves, so just be mindful of how you interact with them. They might just want to keep going since they have a lot of miles left ahead of them. I always like to offer some of

BENEDICT POND

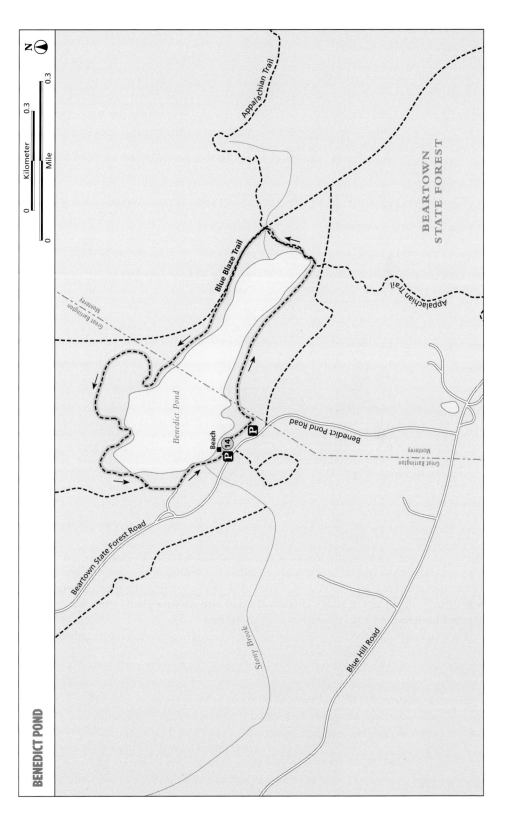

N

Kilometer
0   0.3

Mile
0   0.3

Appalachian Trail

BEARTOWN
STATE FOREST

Appalachian Trail

Blue Blaze Trail

Great Barrington
Monterey

Benedict Pond

Beach

14

Benedict Pond Road

Great Barrington
Monterey

Beartown State Forest Road

Stony Brook

Blue Hill Road

HOW ARE BEAVERS AND HUMANS ALIKE?

There aren't many obvious similarities between beavers and humans. But did you know that beavers are the second closest to humans when it comes to changing the landscape around them to fit their needs? It's true. Sure, humans change their landscape on global scales, erecting enormous buildings and destroying millions of acres of land in the process. Beavers, however, also change their micro-ecosystem, sometimes quite drastically. They're able to cut down trees using their incisor front teeth and use them to build dams where they keep their homes and food stores. Placed in the right area, beaver dams can disrupt massive amounts of water and change the way an area looks in an instant.

my better food—like energy gummies, chocolate granola bars, or trail mix. Many times, thru-hikers eat mostly freeze-dried foods that are light and easy to carry. On trails that I know connect with the Appalachian Trail, I bring full-size candy bars just in case I meet up with a thru-hiker. If not, I just end up eating it.

At the next junction, stay left to head back on the Blue Blaze Trail and round the northern side of the pond. This junction is also where the Appalachian Trail will stay straight and continue on up to Maine. At around the 1.0-mile mark, the trail will start to

The trail has several raised boardwalks to help protect the surrounding wetlands

A view of the pond
along the trail

stray away from the water for a short while. It'll then head back toward the water and to the trailhead, where the beach is located.

MILES AND DIRECTIONS

0.00 Start on the Blue Blaze Trail on the southeastern side of the parking lot.

0.40 Meet up with the Appalachian Trail and white blazes. Turn left onto the Appalachian Trail.

0.50 Turn left to get back on the Blue Blaze Trail as the Appalachian Trail heads straight.

0.70 At the fork, stay left to stick close to the water.

0.90 The trail starts to veer right and away from the water.

1.30 Reach the edge of the pond once again. A small bench is available for you to take in the views.

1.50 Pass by a camping area.

1.70 Arrive back at the trailhead and parking lot. Enjoy the small beach area after your hike to cool off and unwind.

Boardwalks are found throughout
the shaded trail to Benedict Pond

VERMONT

This hidden gem is unknown
to most and is one of the best
swimming holes in this book

15 THE LEDGES

Known to locals as The Ledges, this area along Harriman Reservoir is sure to offer a fun-filled day. The area is well known as a "clothing-optional" place once you cross the small bridge within the Vermont Land Trust boundary, so be prepared for seeing every inch of someone. However, everyone is extremely kind (you're in Vermont after all), and you'll feel right at home even if you choose to keep your bathing suit on.

Start: At the trailhead on the western side of the parking area
Elevation gain: 125 feet
Distance: 1.4 miles out and back
Difficulty: Easy
Hiking time: About 1 hour
Fees and permits: No fee required
Trail contact: Harriman Reservoir, Great River Hydro LLC, 69 Milk St. #306, Westborough, MA 01581; (802) 291-8104; www.greatriverhydro .com/facilities-location/harriman -hydropower-station; and Vermont Land Trust, 8 Bailey Ave., Montpelier, VT 05602; (802) 223-5234; https:// vlt.org

Dog-friendly: Allowed on leash on trails; prohibited in reservoir
Trail surface: Dirt, grass, and rocks/ roots
Land status: Great River Hydro LLC and Vermont Land Trust
Nearest town: Wilmington, VT
Other trail users: None
Temperature of water: 70°F
Body of water: Harriman Reservoir
Water availability: None
Maps: Harriman Reservoir map
Toilets: Yes, down the trail near the water's edge
Wheelchair compatibility: No
Family-friendly: No

FINDING THE TRAILHEAD

From Brattleboro, take VT-9 West/Western Avenue for approximately 18 miles. Turn left onto VT-100 South for just over 1 mile. Turn right onto Boyd Hill Road; the road turns to dirt after 1 mile and changes to Ward's Beach Access Road. Drive 0.3 mile and park in the large parking lot to your right. There is enough parking for dozens of vehicles. GPS: N42 50.0172', W72 52.3992'

THE HIKE

Tucked into southwestern Vermont, The Ledges area is a great place to unwind and swim in a quiet reservoir. From the parking lot, walk down the path next to the kiosks to get down to the boat ramp and picnic area. Here you'll find port-a-potties and several picnic tables with barbecues for visitors to use.

Head right after the port-a-potty and travel along a small trail that keeps the reservoir on your left. There are no blazes on this trail, and you'll likely notice several social trails in this area that are constantly changing. No matter the trail you take, keep close to the water's edge, and always have the reservoir on your left as you make your way out to The Ledges.

Around 0.4 mile, you'll reach a small bridge that is falling apart but still usable to cross the small wetland area. Depending on the year, there might be a lot of water around this place, so be careful. After the bridge, you'll see a sign telling you the rules of the area. This is also where clothing becomes optional, so don't freak out when you see someone

THE LEDGES

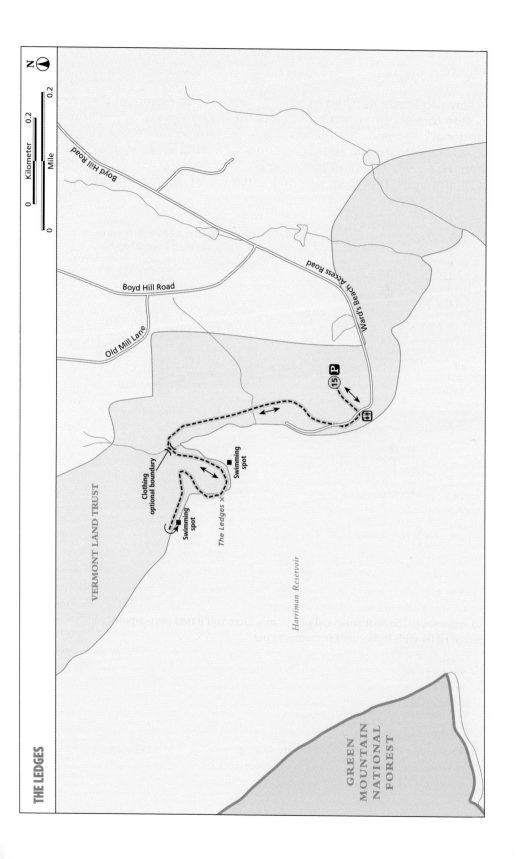

Kilometer
0   0.2

Mile
0   0.2

N

Boyd Hill Road

Boyd Hill Road

Old Mill Lane

Ward's Beach Access Road

15 P

Clothing
optional boundary

Swimming
spot

Swimming
spot

The Ledges ×

VERMONT LAND TRUST

Harriman Reservoir

GREEN
MOUNTAIN
NATIONAL
FOREST

There are a few stream crossings to get to the swimming spots

THE UNDERWATER TOWN OF MOUNTAIN MILLS

Harriman Reservoir (also known as Lake Wilmington) is the largest body of water that completely resides in the state of Vermont. It was also the site of a thriving logging community called Mountain Mills in the early nineteenth century. The settlement had dozens of houses, a water tower, post office, hospital, railroad station, and even a small store.

In 1923 the New England Power Company moved in and used part of the area for its hydroelectric system. Unfortunately, it shifted the way the water table worked in the area, and the town flooded frequently. People left their homes and the town was abandoned soon after the power company moved in. Today you can still see some foundations and old roads when you boat on the reservoir.

walking on the trail with a backpack completely naked. It's allowed here.

The trail splits; I suggest heading toward the left to stay close to the water and see if you can find the first good swimming spot along the trail. If it's crowded or you'd rather keep moving forward, then stay on the trail. This little peninsula of land is where the official Ledges is located as you get to the farthest point into the reservoir. Again, check out the area and see if there's a spot on one of the many ledges for you to lay your towel, or continue on for another swimming hole.

Around the 0.5-mile mark, you'll reach the main trail again. Head left to continue to the next and last swimming hole in the area. If this place is crowded, you might be out of luck for the day. Or try striking up a conversation, since most folks who frequent the area are quite friendly. Once you've had your fill, head back the way you came.

There are several spots along the trail where you can sunbathe on a rock or take a dip in the water

MILES AND DIRECTIONS

0.00   Start at the western end of the parking lot between the kiosks.

0.05   Turn right after the port-a-potty.

0.40   Reach the small bridge and cross into clothing-optional territory.

0.45   Reach the first swimming hole, on your left.

0.50   Reach the official "Ledges" and the second swimming hole.

0.70   Reach the third swimming hole. Go back the way you came.

1.00   Turn right to head over the bridge and back toward the trailhead.

1.35   Turn left when you reach the port-a-potty and head up the slope back to the parking lot.

1.40   Arrive back at the trailhead.

16 WEST DUMMERSTON COVERED BRIDGE

Of the three covered bridge swimming holes in this guide, this one is the longest. The West Dummerston Covered Bridge offers a dramatic skyline to anyone who wants to swim in the waters beneath its wood. This area is particularly good for those with younger ones, as you can wade easily into the water and the flow isn't too strong in most spots along the bank.

Start: At the small parking area on the western bank
Elevation gain: 10 feet
Distance: 0.05 mile out and back (just off the road)
Difficulty: Easy
Hiking time: About 5 minutes
Fees and permits: No fee required
Trail contact: Town of Dummerston, 1523 Middle Rd., East Dummerston, VT 05346; (802) 257-1496; https://dummerston.org

Dog-friendly: Allowed on leash
Trail surface: Pavement and pebbles
Land status: Town of Dummerston
Nearest town: Dummerston, VT
Other trail users: None
Temperature of water: 65°F
Body of water: West River
Water availability: None
Maps: Dummerston road map
Toilets: No
Wheelchair compatibility: No
Family-friendly: Yes

FINDING THE TRAILHEAD
From Brattleboro, take VT-30 North/West River Road for approximately 6 miles. The car park is on the right-hand side of the road, on the western bank of the West River. GPS: N42 56.2188', W72 36.8154'

THE HIKE
I know this section says "the hike," but there is very little hiking involved when getting to the swimming hole beneath the West Dummerston Covered Bridge. It being a covered bridge means there's a road directly nearby and, as such, your hike is quick to the water's edge.

Simply head to the eastern part of the parking lot, where you'll see some stone steps heading down toward the gravel beach. Here you can decide where you'd like to set up your towels and chairs to relax for the day. You can spread out quite a bit even if the parking lot is full. There are places to the left and right, making it easy to snag a secluded spot

A TOUR OF COVERED BRIDGES
Vermont is home to over one hundred covered bridges and has the highest density of covered bridges of all the states. If you're feeling whimsical and want to see these timeless architectural wonders, start at West Dummerston and work your way north and east along the Connecticut River corridor, where a large number of bridges are located. For the locations of all the covered bridges in Vermont, check out the following website: www.vermontvacation .com/things-to-do/arts-and-heritage/covered-bridges.

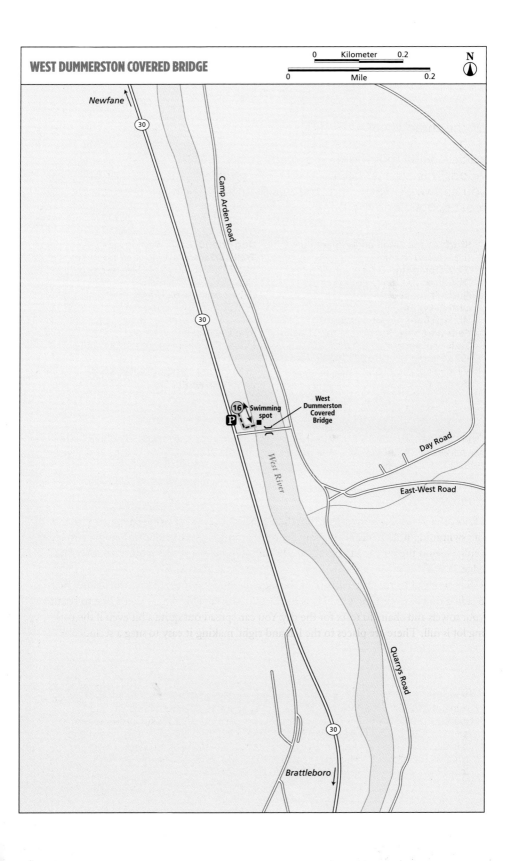

0   Kilometer   0.2

0   Mile   0.2

N

Newfane

30

Camp Arden Road

30

16   Swimming
          spot

P

West
Dummerston
Covered
Bridge

Day Road

West River

East-West Road

Quarry's Road

30

Brattleboro

The parking lot is very close to
the path to the beach area

West Dummerston Covered Bridge is a gorgeous backdrop to the swimming hole

for you and your companions. Enjoy wading in the river or sunbathing on the gravel/coarse sand banks.

This spot is ideal for little ones who want to sit in the water without the threat of being swept downriver. The flow here is at a much slower pace than at many of the other rivers in this guide. As is the case when visiting any swimming hole with little kids, always keep an eye on them to make sure they are playing safely.

MILES AND DIRECTIONS

0.00 Start at the eastern end of the parking lot. Head down the steps to the gravel beach.

0.02 Reach the gravel beach. Go back the way you came.

0.04 Arrive back at the parking lot.

17 ANGEL FALLS

This swimming hole is for anyone willing to work just a bit to find one of the best swimming holes in New England. Angel Falls was a pleasant surprise and one I won't soon forget. It's not a well-known spot, so the small pool at the base of the falls will do just fine if you're hiking in by yourself. Enjoy the views of the West River while basking in the spray from the falls.

Start: At the trailhead southwest of the gazebo
Elevation gain: 400 feet
Distance: 1.5 miles out and back
Difficulty: Easy to moderate (due to elevation)
Hiking time: About 1 hour
Fees and permits: No fee required
Trail contact: West River Trail, Upper Section, PO Box 2086, South Londonderry, VT 05155; https://westrivertrail.org; and US Army Corps of Engineers New England District, 88 Ball Mountain Ln., Jamaica, VT 05343; (978) 318-8914; www.nae.usace.army.mil/missions/recreation/ball-mountain-lake

Dog-friendly: Allowed on leash
Trail surface: Dirt and rocks/roots
Land status: Friends of the West River Trail and US Army Corps of Engineers
Nearest town: Jamaica, VT
Other trail users: None
Temperature of water: 65°F
Body of water: Tributary of the West River
Water availability: None
Maps: West River Trail map
Toilets: No
Wheelchair compatibility: No
Family-friendly: Yes

FINDING THE TRAILHEAD
From Brattleboro, take VT-30 North/West River Road for approximately 26 miles. Turn right onto Ball Mountain Lane and continue for just under a mile. You will see a gazebo and picnic area on your left and a small parking area on your right. Park in one of the 6 parking spots. GPS: N43 7.1742', W72 47.535'

THE HIKE
Start your hike just south of the picnic area and gazebo across from the small parking lot. You'll see a small gap in the guardrail and a hiker sign indicating that the trail dips down here. Immediately, you descend quickly to get closer to the river's edge. You'll traverse through a young hardwood forest full of American beeches, maples, and oaks.

As the trail levels out, you'll reach the junction with the West River Trail. This trail was once the location of a 36-mile railroad route between Brattleboro and Londonderry. The track shut down over seventy-five years ago, but sections of the route are now used for recreational opportunities. The upper section is complete, while the lower section is still in the works to be acquired by Friends of the West River Trail.

Turn left on the West River Trail, where you'll start to get glimpses of the river to your right. You'll wind up and down along the trail through an older-growth cedar forest until you reach an opening around the 0.6-mile mark. This area is flanked by blackberry bushes and angelica plants right up until you reach the falls.

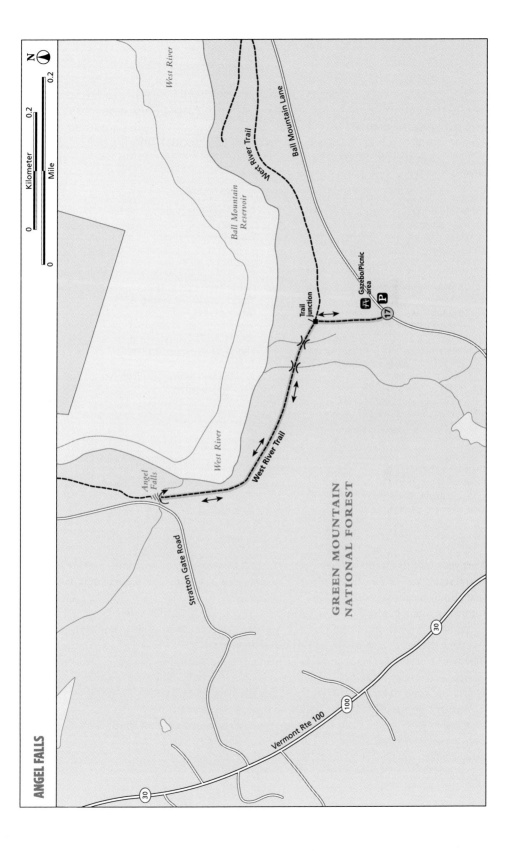

ANGEL FALLS

West River

West River

Ball Mountain Reservoir

West River Trail

Ball Mountain Lane

Trail Junction

Gazebo/Picnic area

P

17

West River

Angel Falls

Stratton Gate Road

West River Trail

GREEN MOUNTAIN NATIONAL FOREST

Vermont Rte 100

30

100

30

N

Kilometer
0   0.2   0.2

Mile
0   0.2

From here, it's another 0.1 mile until you reach the falls. They'll be on your left, and it's best to cross the small river using the rocks that have been positioned across the water to get a better view. You can lay your gear to the side and strip down to your bathing suit to dip into the pool here. The small pool feels like heaven on a hot day along the trail. Angel Falls is a series of cascades over huge, jagged boulders that fall about 25 feet and fan out before being split in two by a large rock.

The trail descends steeply from the road and into the river valley below

The trailhead starts just to the left of this gazebo and is a great place to rest after the hike

Depending on the month you go, you might see butterflies flittering about. They're likely the red-spotted admirals, which are very common in the area. From the pool, you can also check out the view down to the West River and beyond to the Green Mountains across the way.

When you're finished swimming (and believe me, you likely will be here awhile), head back the way you came. Don't forget to take the right off West River Trail to ensure you make it back to the correct parking lot. It'll be steep on the way back, so take your time. At the end, grab a lunch or snack and relax in the gazebo before you head out.

MILES AND DIRECTIONS

- 0.00 Start at the trailhead just south of the gazebo/picnic area.
- 0.15 Reach the junction with the West River Trail. Take a left to head west.
- 0.60 Reach the southern edge of an open area flanked by blackberry bushes and angelica plants.
- 0.75 Arrive at Angel Falls. Relax and then head back the way you came.
- 0.90 Reach the edge of the old-growth cedar forest.
- 1.35 Take a right off West River Trail and onto the trail that brings you back to your car. It will be steep all the way back to the road.
- 1.50 Arrive back at the trailhead and gazebo/picnic area.

18 MAD TOM FALLS

Don't worry—this trail won't make you go crazy, but it could put you in a complete sense of calm due to its tranquility. Mad Tom Falls isn't anything spectacular, but the pool beneath the uppermost falls is breathtaking. The deep pool has crystal-clear waters that give off that signature green hue due to the granite that lies beneath it. The falls are calm enough that the water isn't churning with whirls.

Start: At the East Dorset trailhead
Elevation gain: 160 feet
Distance: 1.0 mile out and back
Difficulty: Easy
Hiking time: About 30 minutes
Fees and permits: No fee required
Trail contact: Green Mountain National Forest, 2538 Depot St., Manchester, VT 05255; (802) 362-2307; www.fs.usda.gov/gmfl
Dog-friendly: Allowed on leash
Trail surface: Dirt and rocks/roots

Land status: US Forest Service—Green Mountain National Forest
Nearest town: East Dorset, VT
Other trail users: None
Temperature of water: 65°F
Body of water: Mad Tom Brook
Water availability: None
Maps: Mad Tom Brook area map
Toilets: No
Wheelchair compatibility: No
Family-friendly: Yes

FINDING THE TRAILHEAD

From Brattleboro, take VT-30 North/West River Road for approximately 20 miles. Turn right onto Windham Hill Road and continue for approximately 8 miles. Turn left onto VT-121 West for 2 miles, then turn left onto VT-11 West. Continue on VT-11 West for approximately 18 miles. Take a slight right onto the ramp to Rutland and merge onto US-7 North. Follow US-7 North for approximately 5 miles and then turn right onto Mad Tom Road. Where the road forks, go straight/to the right onto the dirt road to the small parking lot for the trailhead. There is parking for around 10 vehicles. GPS: N43 14.4384', W72 59.886'

THE HIKE

The hike starts just past the big boulders that line the eastern part of the parking lot to prevent cars from going any farther. The trail is identified with blue blazes along an old logging road. There is a trail off to the right not too far down the trail, but you continue straight toward the brook.

This trail was likely used for travel and hunting access by the Native Americans who lived here prior to European settlement. It was then used by settlers to walk to town hall meetings and other events. Once the trail was taken over by the town of Mount Tabor, it transported people and goods up to the Notch while birch trees were felled and sent down the lumber spout for construction of the Rutland Railroad. It became even more heavily logged during the mid-1800s until a huge portion of the road was taken out due to heavy rainfall and flooding. It was then rebuilt and used to transport goods until it was destroyed again in a flood in 1927 and yet again in 2011 by Hurricane Irene. It wasn't until 2017 that the hiking trail—now called East Dorset Trail—was completed.

Continuing on after the history lesson, there is a fork in the trail at the 0.15-mile mark; veer right here. You'll reach the lower falls at the 0.3-mile mark. This isn't a

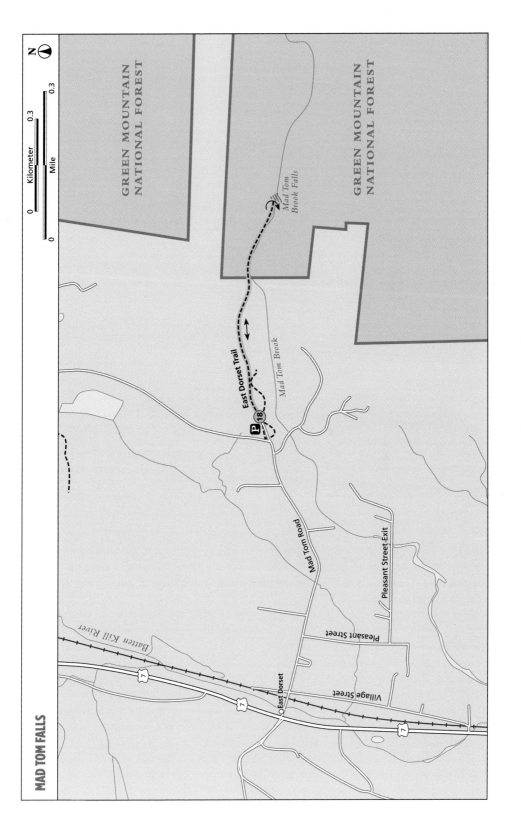

MAD TOM FALLS

GREEN MOUNTAIN NATIONAL FOREST

GREEN MOUNTAIN NATIONAL FOREST

Mad Tom Brook Falls

East Dorset Trail

Mad Tom Brook

P 18

Mad Tom Road

Pleasant Street Exit

Pleasant Street

Village Street

East Dorset

Batten Kill River

N

Kilometer
0   0.3

Mile
0   0.3

WHY IT'S CALLED MAD TOM BROOK

Historians have tried to figure out why the brook was named "Mad Tom" but have yet to come to a conclusion. The "Tom" part is baffling, as there are no significant persons in history in the area named Tom. They have, however, deduced that the "Mad" part of the name is likely due to the nature of the brook itself and not some sort of mental diagnosis of the person it's named for. The brook can turn into a raging river with even the smallest amount of rainfall. The landscape can change so drastically that people who have adventured here more than once often notice many changes throughout the brook.

great spot for swimming since it doesn't really have a pool and is very shallow. Farther downstream there are some great spots for younger kiddos who just want to wade in the brook.

Certain times of year, the mosquitoes are terrible here. The whole brook is shaded with trees, which keeps moisture close to the ground. This creates a haven for mosquitoes and an awful experience for hikers. Luckily for you, they seem to avoid the pools.

There's a wide and easy path to get to the falls

Although the falls aren't huge, the pools are still refreshing to swim in

The next set of cascades occurs about 300 feet upstream and is only about 4 feet tall. The uppermost falls are another 200 feet upstream from the middle cascades. This is your best bet at a good swimming hole. There's a big boulder perfect to sit and lounge on while waiting to jump into the pool underneath the small waterfalls of the uppermost cascade.

MILES AND DIRECTIONS

0.00 Start at the East Dorset trailhead, just past the big boulders in the parking lot. Ignore the trail to the right and continue straight on the old logging road (follow the blue blazes).

0.15 Veer right.

0.30 Reach the lower falls.

0.40 Reach the middle falls.

0.50 Reach the upper falls. Turn back the way you came when you're finished swimming.

0.85 Veer left to head toward the parking lot.

1.00 Arrive back at the trailhead.

19 DORSET MARBLE QUARRY

It isn't often you get to jump 50 feet into a clear, deep pool in the middle of a marble quarry. But it turns out you can when you visit Dorset Marble Quarry. Owned and operated by a private local party, this parcel of land has been a hidden gem in Vermont for many decades. It remains open to the public, so make sure to keep this place clean and pristine for more generations to enjoy.

Start: At the quarry's large parking area
Elevation gain: None
Distance: None
Difficulty: Easy
Hiking time: None
Fees and permits: Parking fee and registration required
Trail contact: Dorset Marble Quarry, 1848 VT-30, Dorset, VT 05251; (802) 566-0677; https://dorsetquarry.com
Dog-friendly: Allowed on leash
Trail surface: Grass and marble slabs
Land status: Privately owned
Nearest town: Dorset, VT
Other trail users: None
Temperature of water: 70°F
Body of water: Dorset Marble Quarry
Water availability: None
Maps: None
Toilets: Yes, at the parking area
Wheelchair compatibility: No
Family-friendly: Yes

FINDING THE TRAILHEAD
From Manchester, take VT-30 North/Bonnet Street for approximately 5 miles. Pull into the large parking lot and make sure to check in with the attendant. GPS: N43 14.2092', W73 5.0346'

THE HIKE
There isn't much of a hike when you visit Dorset Quarry. The swimming hole is just off VT-30 and easily accessible for many people visiting the area. The quarry is a popular hangout among high schoolers and can get rowdy at times. The owners are usually on the property managing the site to make sure that everyone is recreating safely without disturbing others.

You can walk around to the other side of the quarry along the stone wall that traverses the property or simply jump in and swim to the other side. There are ladders to help people get in and out of the quarry. The cliffs on the far side of the quarry are used frequently by thrill-seekers to jump from. They rise more than 30 feet out of the water. As long as you jump far enough away from the cliffs, you'll be safe, as the bottom of the quarry pool lies 60 feet below the water.

Fish and other aquatic life can be found in the water. If you feel something tickling your feet, it's likely just a fish saying hello rather than a monster reaching for its prey from the depths below. I'll be honest, though—jumping into this pool can be scary, especially for those of you (like me) who have thalassophobia (see sidebar for the definition of this term).

Dorset Marble Quarry was the state's, and likely the nation's, first commercial marble quarry. Isaac Underhill and Reuben Bloomer started manufacturing headstones back in

DORSET MARBLE QUARRY

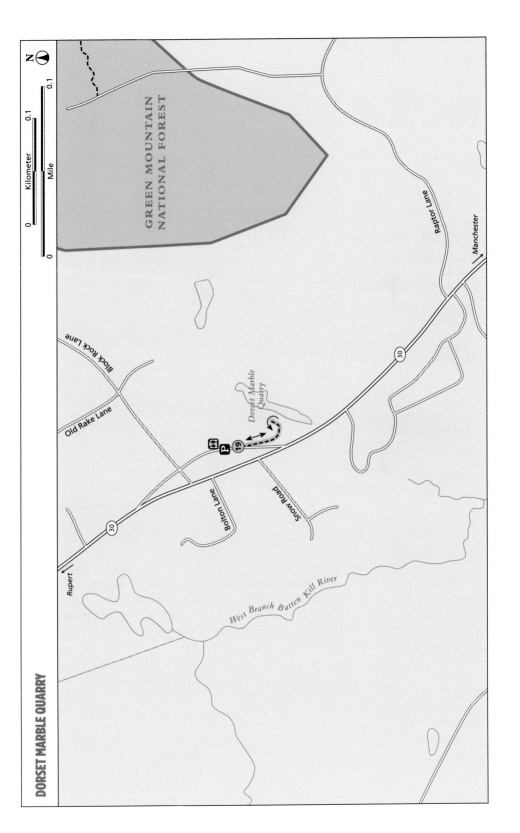

GREEN MOUNTAIN
NATIONAL FOREST

Black Rock Lane

Old Rake Lane

Dorset Marble
Quarry

Bolton Lane

Snow Road

West Branch Batten Kill River

Raptor Lane

Manchester

Rupert

N

Kilometer
0   0.1   0.1

Mile
0   0.1

Jumping from the surrounding cliffs is
allowed due to the depth of the pool

On a hot summer day, this is a popular spot for locals and visitors alike

1785. More quarries opened up along the slopes of Dorset Mountain, which was soon overrun with small blocks for headstones, hearths, and more.

Since it opened, Dorset Marble Quarry has helped build some of the most notable pieces of architecture in the nation, including the New York Public Library, Harvard Medical School, and Montreal's Museum of Fine Art. It eventually closed to commercial mining in 1920 and became a popular swimming hole just two years later. It recently celebrated its one hundredth anniversary as a local swimming spot.

MILES AND DIRECTIONS

0.00   The quarry is just past the parking lot and takes zero effort to walk to the water's edge.

THALASSOPHOBIANS AND WHAT THEY'RE AFRAID OF

I hadn't ever heard the exact name of the condition, but I knew I was afraid of water where I couldn't see the bottom. As an author, I have an overactive imagination, and it runs rampant when I'm in water. When I can't see what's below me, my heart rate kicks up and my breathing gets labored. I'm not exactly sure what I'm so afraid of, but I now know there's a term for this fear. It's called thalassophobia. Technically, it refers to the fear of the ocean or other deep bodies of water. Sometimes, the fear also involves the creatures that typically dwell in deep bodies of water. If you are like me and suffer from the same fear, this quarry might not be the best swimming hole option for you.

20 BUTTERMILK FALLS

Buttermilk Falls is one of the more popular swimming holes in this guide. But the pools are just too good not to include them here. There are three distinct waterfalls and pools, each with its own personality. Although the middle and upper falls are something to behold, don't miss out on the lower falls, where very few venture. You might be in for a surprise.

Start: Off Buttermilk Falls Road
Elevation gain: 50 feet
Distance: 0.5 mile out and back
Difficulty: Easy
Hiking time: About 15 minutes
Fees and permits: No fee required
Trail contact: Okemo State Forest, 100 Mineral St., Ste. 304, Springfield, VT 05156; (802) 289-0613; https://fpr.vermont.gov/okemo-state-forest; and Vermont River Conservancy, 29 Main St., Ste. 11, Montpelier, VT 05602; (802) 229-0820; https://vermontriverconservancy.org

Dog-friendly: Allowed on leash
Trail surface: Dirt and rocks/roots
Land status: Vermont Department of Forests, Parks, and Recreation and Vermont River Conservancy
Nearest town: Ludlow, VT
Other trail users: None
Temperature of water: 65°F
Body of water: Branch Brook
Water availability: None
Maps: Okemo State Forest map
Toilets: No
Wheelchair compatibility: No
Family-friendly: Yes

FINDING THE TRAILHEAD

From Brattleboro, take I-91 North for approximately 23 miles. Take exit 6 for US-5 toward Rockingham/VT-103/Rutland. Turn left onto US-5 North and then take a slight left onto VT-103 North. Continue for approximately 24 miles, then turn right onto Buttermilk Falls Road. Parking can be found on the side of the road at both the lower and upper falls. GPS: N43 26.1198', W72 43.6122'

THE HIKE

Most New Englanders might know this area for the large ski resort that the mountain houses, but it's also where Buttermilk Falls resides. The start of the trail begins on the side of Buttermilk Falls Road. You are allowed to park on the sides of the road as long as you are not impeding traffic. This hike starts at the lower falls and goes to the upper falls; however, you could also park at the upper falls and work your way down, or simply hang out at whatever falls you like.

Each falls is unique in its own way. The lowermost falls is small compared to the other ones, but still provides a beautiful pool beneath. The water is tinted green like many pools in the area due to the underlying parent material (i.e., granite). The lower falls is also usually the least crowded since the pool is shallower and the falls not as spectacular.

The middle falls has a 20-foot drop into a 25-foot-wide pool below. It's an ideal spot for swimming in the wilderness. Unfortunately, many other people know about this place, so you likely won't have it to yourself. The upper falls is somewhat similar to the middle one and is a segmented horsetail falls. It also lands into a wide pool at the bottom that is a favorite among visitors to the area.

BUTTERMILK FALLS

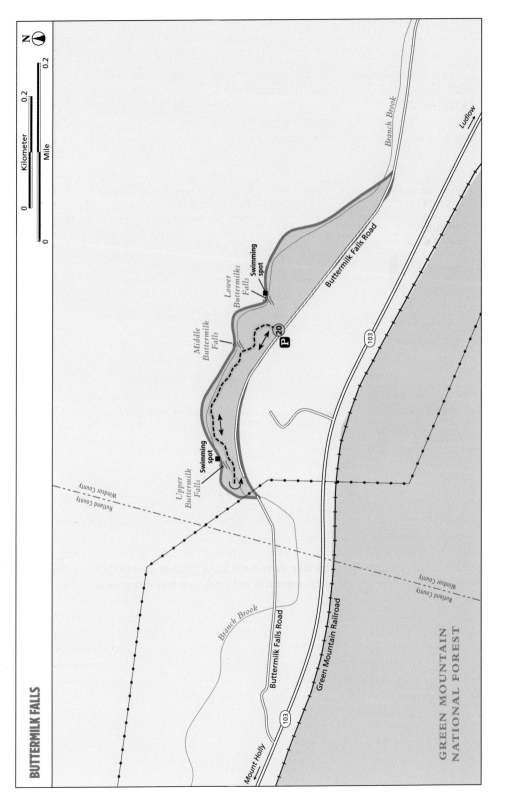

Mount Holly

Branch Brook

Buttermilk Falls Road

Green Mountain Railroad

103

Rutland County
Windsor County

Upper
Buttermilk
Falls

Swimming
spot

Middle
Buttermilk
Falls

Lower
Buttermilk
Falls

Swimming
spot

20

P

Rutland County
Windsor County

103

Buttermilk Falls Road

Branch Brook

Ludlow

GREEN MOUNTAIN
NATIONAL FOREST

N

0   0.2
Kilometer
0   0.2
Mile

The upper falls of
Buttermilk Falls

The upper falls cascade down jagged
rocks—be careful stepping over here

VERMONT HAS A HISTORY OF MERINO WOOL

Many outdoor enthusiasts know the term "merino wool," the pricey garment material that is often likely the reason for a drained bank account. But did you know that Vermont has some early history on the making of merino wool? Merino wool is a thinner and softer version of regular wool and is used abundantly in the outdoor industry. It keeps you warm and dry—something that can prevent a lot of injuries and illness in the backcountry. But back in the early 1800s, Vermont was one of the first states to bring over merino sheep and begin milling and weaving the wool to make a profit.

When you're finished examining each of the different waterfalls, select the one that's best for you and stay awhile. Then head back up one of the many trails to the road and where your car is parked.

MILES AND DIRECTIONS

0.00 Start at the side of Buttermilk Falls Road at the lower falls. When you reach the water's edge, the lower falls are off to the right.

0.05 Reach Middle Buttermilk Falls.

0.25 Reach the upper falls. Turn around and head back the way you came to your car.

0.50 Arrive back at the trailhead.

21 CLARENDON GORGE

This is one of those trails where you can choose to do the longer route or simply walk the few hundred feet to the swimming hole and be done. I highly recommend heading out on the long hike to get the full experience and then reward yourself with a cool dip in the stream. If you opt for the longer hike, you'll travel along the Long Trail—a 272-mile traverse along the main ridge of Green Mountain National Forest. It is the oldest continuous footpath in the United States and a sight that many come to experience.

Start: At the Long Trail trailhead
Elevation gain: Up to 2,550 feet
Distance: Up to 10.0 miles out and back
Difficulty: Easy to strenuous, depending on length
Hiking time: Up to 5 hours
Fees and permits: No fee required
Trail contact: US Forest Service, Green Mountain & Finger Lakes National Forests, PO Box 220, Rutland, VT 05702; (802) 747-6700; www.greenmountainclub.org/the -long-trail
Dog-friendly: Allowed on leash

Trail surface: Dirt
Land status: US Forest Service— Green Mountain National Forest
Nearest town: Clarendon, VT
Other trail users: None
Temperature of water: 65°F
Body of water: Mill River
Water availability: None
Maps: Long Trail map—Upper Falls section
Toilets: No
Wheelchair compatibility: No
Family-friendly: Yes, in some spots, but many high rocks to easily fall from

FINDING THE TRAILHEAD

From Lebanon, New Hampshire, take I-91 South for 18.6 miles. Take exit 8 for VT-131 toward US-5/VT-12. Turn right onto VT-131 West for 16 miles and then turn right onto VT-103 North for approximately 20 miles. Look for signs for Long Trail parking on your left and pull into the parking lot. GPS: N43 31.2774', W72 55.5096'

THE HIKE

Start your hike at the northern tip of this out-and-back trail. When you've parked, head over to the kiosk and look for any alerts in the area before making your way down the narrow path to the suspension bridge. Any weather or water alerts are posted at the kiosk, so don't forget to check it out. If all is clear, then head out.

Within just 0.1 mile, the suspension bridge will come into view. If you've got kids with you, make sure to watch them as they go across the bridge. There is no way for a child to accidentally fall from the bridge since it's completely fenced in, but be careful regardless.

Once you are across the bridge, you can choose to continue on the Long Trail or stop here to check out the swimming hole. If it's the latter, traverse down the path to your left to head to the river below. The rocks can be extremely slippery when wet, so take care in this area. More adventurous souls can continue on the Long Trail to do the full 10.0 miles.

Green Mountain National Forest is called "Green" because of the trees that blanket the entire area, including the mountain summits (unlike the White Mountains of New

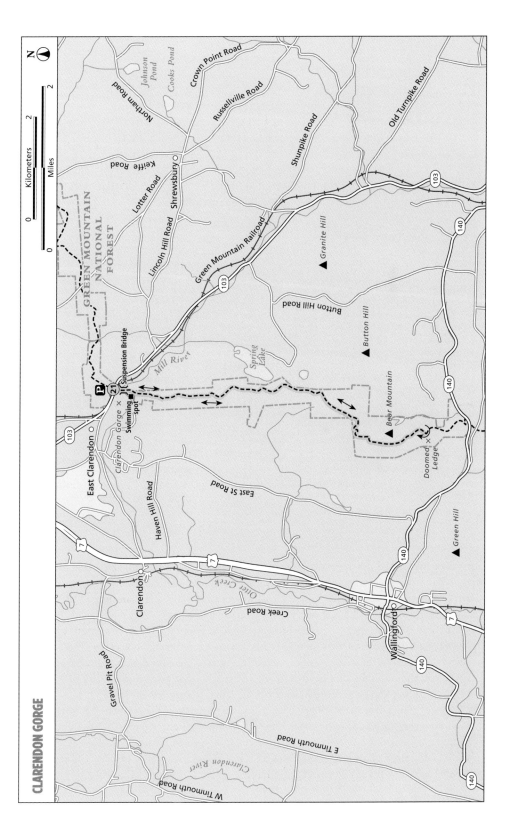

CLARENDON GORGE

N

| Kilometers | 0 | 2 |
| Miles | 0 | 2 |

GREEN MOUNTAIN NATIONAL FOREST

Johnson Pond

Cooks Pond

Northam Road

Crown Point Road

Russellville Road

Keiffe Road

Lotter Road

Shrewsbury

Lincoln Hill Road

Shunpike Road

Old Turnpike Road

Green Mountain Railroad

103

140

Granite Hill ▲

Button Hill Road

Button Hill ▲

Suspension Bridge

Mill River

Spring Lake

Bear Mountain ▲

P 21

East Clarendon

103

Clarendon Gorge ×
Swimming spot

Haven Hill Road

East St Road

Doomed Ledge ×

140

Green Hill ▲

7

Clarendon

Otter Creek

Creek Road

Wallingford

140

7

Gravel Pit Road

E Timmouth Road

W Timmouth Road

Clarendon River

Swimming is perfect just under and upstream of the suspension bridge

Balancing rocks is popular in this area, but try not to build more as it disrupts the flow of the river

Hampshire). You'll traverse through hemlock and pine forest as well as beech, birch, and maple stands.

Nearly 4.5 miles from the start, you will reach the summit of Bear Mountain, which stands 2,231 feet above sea level. Unfortunately, like many summits in Green Mountain National Forest, the view is obscured by trees. Head down the trail another 0.75 mile to Doomed Ledge, a rocky outcrop with a vista looking southwest.

You can keep hiking south to VT-140 if you've got a car shuttle to bring you back to the car you parked off VT-103. If not, head back the way you came. The hike back can feel long, but keep that pep in your step since a glorious swimming hole is waiting for you back at the start of the trailhead.

MILES AND DIRECTIONS

0.00 Start at the parking lot and hike south on the Long Trail.

0.10 Head over the suspension bridge.

4.30 Reach the summit of Bear Mountain.

SECTION-HIKING VERSUS THRU-HIKING

Many outdoor enthusiasts have heard the terms "section-hiking" and "thru-hiking." But what exactly is the difference? Thru-hiking is what you often see in movies and on the news. The film *Wild* with Reese Witherspoon depicts Cheryl Strayed's thru-hiking experience along the Pacific Crest Trail.

Thru-hiking simply means hiking a long-distance trail in one go. For instance, thousands of hikers start in April down in Georgia to try their hand (or should I say "foot") at hiking the Appalachian Trail, which heads all the way up to Mount Katahdin in Maine. However, not everyone can nor desires to hike 2,000-plus miles in one fell swoop. Instead, they'll do sections over time. This is called section-hiking. Hikers can do a little bit here and there, not necessarily in geographic order, but still finish the entirety of the Appalachian Trail without having to take months off work.

The suspension bridge over Clarendon Gorge

5.05   Reach Doomed Ledge. Turn around here, or continue south to VT-140 if you have a car/shuttle waiting for you.

5.80   Reach the summit of Bear Mountain again; continue north on the trail.

9.90   Head back over the suspension bridge.

10.00 Arrive back at the trailhead.

22 FALLS OF LANA

Be prepared for such stunning falls that you'll want to learn how to paint afterward. These falls are unlike any of the other ones in this guide. The upper falls plunges deep into a gorge and ends in a beautiful pool to swim in. For those willing to go the extra mile (although it's more like 0.8 mile), you'll be rewarded with two more majestic waterfalls with incredible pools for swimming.

Start: At the Falls of Lana trailhead
Elevation gain: 300 feet
Distance: 1.4 miles out and back
Difficulty: Easy to moderate
(scrambling at the end)
Hiking time: About 1 hour
Fees and permits: Fee required
Trail contact: Moosalamoo National
Recreation Area, Green Mountain
& Finger Lakes National Forests,
PO Box 220, Rutland, VT 05702;
(802) 747-6700; www.fs.usda
.gov/recarea/gmfl/recreation/
recarea/?recid=64903

Dog-friendly: Allowed on leash
Trail surface: Dirt and rocks/roots
Land status: US Forest Service
Nearest town: Salisbury, VT
Other trail users: None
Temperature of water: 60°F
Body of water: Sucker Brook
Water availability: None
Maps: Green Mountain National
Forest map
Toilets: No
Wheelchair compatibility: No
Family-friendly: No

FINDING THE TRAILHEAD

From Burlington, take US-7 South for approximately 40 miles. Turn left onto VT-53/Lake Dunmore Road. Follow this road for almost 4 miles and then turn left into the parking lot. If you are using a GPS to get directions, just know that the route it may take you on is not actually a road that public vehicles can take. The trailhead is just off VT-53/Lake Dunmore Road. GPS: N43 54.0132′, W73 3.8436′

THE HIKE

The trail starts right at the parking area off VT-53/Lake Dunmore Road. It's an obvious trail that goes up a set of stone stairs and starts to ascend into the trees. After a few hundred feet, you'll take a right onto a dirt road to head uphill some more.

You'll reach a large pipeline in a clearing at around 0.3 mile. This is the Silver Lake Penstock line, which controls the water flow within the lake to ensure flooding doesn't occur. Pass underneath the pipe, where you'll have two options: You can either continue on this trail to head toward the swimming hole at the base of the upper falls or take a left down a well-worn path to take in the views of the middle falls.

If you choose the latter, make your way down about 200 feet until you reach a fence alongside a cliff where you can view the falls. Then head back up to the main trail. In another few hundred feet, look for another trail off to the left, which will lead you to the observation area for the upper falls. You are free to take this trail or keep on the main trail to get to your primary destination.

Around the 0.5-mile mark, you'll cross over Sucker Brook on a wooden bridge and then immediately hang a left. This brings you off the main trail and into a more rugged part of the area. It isn't technically a trail, so only stick to the places that have already

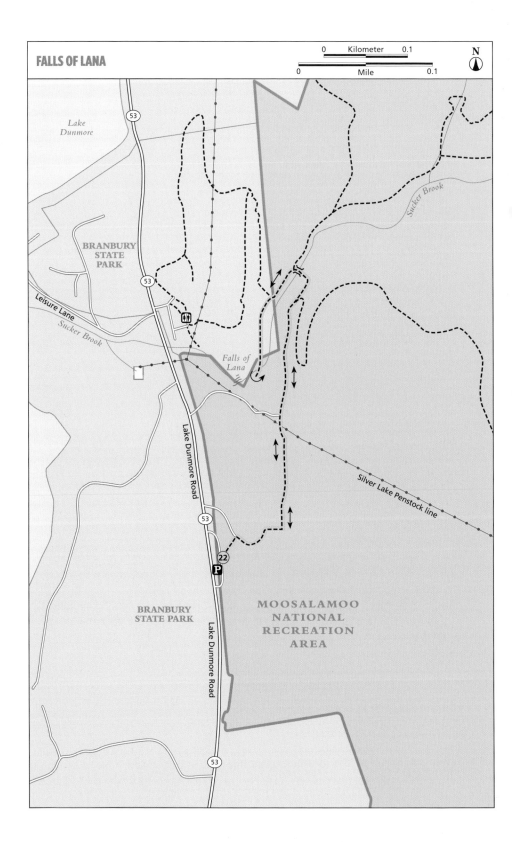

0   Kilometer   0.1

0   Mile   0.1

N

Lake
Dunmore

53

BRANBURY
STATE
PARK

53

Leisure Lane

Sucker Brook

Falls of
Lana

Sucker Brook

Lake Dunmore Road

53

22

P

Silver Lake Penstock line

BRANBURY
STATE PARK

Lake Dunmore Road

MOOSALAMOO
NATIONAL
RECREATION
AREA

53

The trail is an old logging road wide enough for anyone to pass you

been traveled on. You'll take this trail for approximately 0.2 mile until you reach a rock scramble to get down to the pool at the upper falls. A fall from this height would likely be fatal, so tread carefully and never attempt in slippery conditions.

Once you get down, you'll have the pool to wade into with very few people around. I think because it takes quite a bit of effort to get there, not many people venture this far. Enjoy your time at this remarkable swimming hole, then head back up the rock scramble and onto the main trail once again. If you've brought a lunch, there is a backcountry picnic area for you to enjoy a snack before heading back to your car.

WHERE DO THE GREEN MOUNTAINS GET THEIR NAME?

There's no real secret as to the reasoning behind why the Green Mountains are called the Green Mountains. They are, in fact, green. Unlike the White Mountains to the east, the Green Mountains of Vermont mostly have tree-covered summits. Sure, in the winter, they might be called the Brown Mountains, but every spring the trees bloom yet again and blanket the state in a sea of green. Vermont is the fourth most forested state in the country.

MILES AND DIRECTIONS

0.00 Begin at the Silver Lake Trail and head uphill.

0.03 Take a right to follow the dirt road uphill.

The pools above Falls of Lana are great swimming spots

0.30 Cross under the Silver Lake Penstock line. Turn left down a well-worn trail if you want to view the middle falls. Otherwise, continue on the same path.

0.35 You can take a left to view the upper falls or continue on the trail to reach the swimming holes.

0.50 Cross over Sucker Brook using the wooden bridge. Hang a left when you reach the other side.

0.70 Reach the base of the upper falls by scrambling down a steep rock wall. Climb back up when you are done in the pool.

0.90 Cross back over the wooden bridge.

1.10 Go under the Silver Lake Penstock line again.

1.40 Arrive back at the trailhead.

23 BARTLETT AND BRISTOL FALLS

With two crowded swimming holes popular among locals and visitors alike, Bartlett and Bristol Falls still don't disappoint. Due to their large expanse, both falls are great for those not wanting to head into the backcountry but still desiring a bit of ruggedness in their swimming holes.

Start: Off Lincoln Road at the junction with VT-116
Elevation gain: 40 feet
Distance: 0.3 mile out and back
Difficulty: Easy
Hiking time: About 5 minutes
Fees and permits: No fee required
Trail contact: Green Mountain & Finger Lakes National Forests, PO Box 220, Rutland, VT 05702; (802) 747-6700; www.fs.usda.gov/recarea/gmfl
Dog-friendly: Allowed on leash

Trail surface: Pavement, dirt, and rocks/roots
Land status: US Forest Service
Nearest town: Bristol, VT
Other trail users: None
Temperature of water: 65°F
Body of water: New Haven River
Water availability: None
Maps: Green Mountain National Forest map
Toilets: No
Wheelchair compatibility: No
Family-friendly: Yes

FINDING THE TRAILHEAD

From Burlington, take I-89 South for approximately 5 miles. Take exit 12 for VT-2A toward US-2/VT-116/Williston/Essex Junction. Turn right onto VT-2A South and continue for 5 miles. Turn left onto VT-116 South and continue for approximately 18 miles. Turn left onto Lincoln Road. Parking is available along the right-hand side of Lincoln Road. The largest area to park is right when you turn onto Lincoln Road. This is where you'll find Bristol Falls. Bartlett Falls is a little farther up the road. GPS: N44 7.6986', W73 2.958'

THE HIKE

All along Lincoln Road, you can pull over and park your car, so if you don't want to "hike" at all, you don't have to. I prefer to park at Bristol Falls, which is immediately on the right-hand side of Lincoln Road as you turn off VT-17/116. This is more of an official parking area rather than just pulling off to the side of the road.

Head down one of the many social trails that descend quickly to the river's edge. You'll likely see loads of people hanging around, especially on hot weekend days. Luckily, the pools and waterfalls are large enough that they can accommodate a lot of people, so you won't feel too crowded.

You can also head uphill along the road to check out Bartlett Falls and see if it's any less crowded. There is some confusion as to what exactly these waterfalls are called. Most people call both of them Bartlett Falls, while others call them Bartlett Falls and Bristol Falls as if they were two distinct sets of waterfalls. I personally have no preference because both swimming holes are glorious and that's all that really matters.

There are several ledges that you could potentially jump from, but I'd personally stay away from doing that. The pool is fairly deep, but I still wouldn't risk jumping. Instead,

BARTLETT AND BRISTOL FALLS

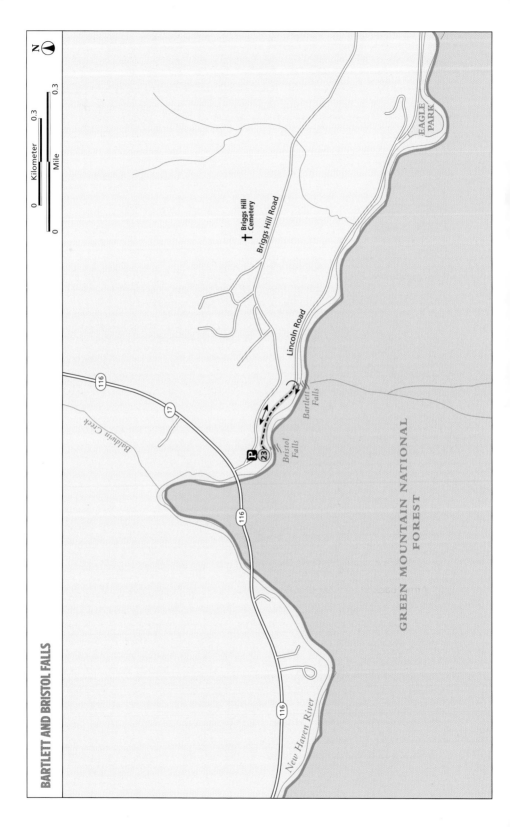

N

0   Kilometer   0.3

0   Mile   0.3

Baldwin Creek

116

17

116

New Haven River

116

Briggs Hill
Cemetery

Briggs Hill Road

Lincoln Road

P
23

Bristol
Falls

Bartlett
Falls

GREEN MOUNTAIN NATIONAL
FOREST

EAGLE
PARK

Bartlett Falls from atop the cliffs surrounding New Haven River

use the ledges to lay out your towels and sunbathe in between taking dips in the cool water.

MILES AND DIRECTIONS

0.00 Start at the large parking lot off Lincoln Road near Bristol Falls. Look for a small trail that heads down to the falls. When you've had your fill of Bristol Falls, head back up to the road and walk to Bartlett Falls.

0.15 Reach Bartlett Falls. Again, a small trail goes down to the water's edge. Head back up to the road when you're finished.

0.30 Arrive back at your car near Bristol Falls.

24 WARREN FALLS

When you see photos of Warren Falls, you likely won't believe the color of the water. But I'm telling you—these pictures are not edited to enhance any colors. The water truly is this emerald-green, crystal-clear color that you only dream about. And with the large, flat ledges that flank the sides of the river, it's easy to get lost in a daydream.

Start: Off VT-100
Elevation gain: 15 feet
Distance: 0.25 mile out and back
Difficulty: Easy
Hiking time: About 5 minutes
Fees and permits: No fee required
Trail contact: Green Mountain & Finger Lakes National Forests, PO Box 220, Rutland, VT 05702; (802) 747-6700; www.fs.usda.gov/recarea/gmfl
Dog-friendly: Allowed on leash

Trail surface: Granite slabs, dirt, and rocks/roots
Land status: US Forest Service
Nearest town: Warren, VT
Other trail users: None
Temperature of water: 65°F
Body of water: Mad River
Water availability: None
Maps: Green Mountain National Forest map
Toilets: No
Wheelchair compatibility: No
Family-friendly: Yes

FINDING THE TRAILHEAD

From Burlington, take I-89 South for approximately 24 miles. Take exit 10 to merge onto VT-100 South/Waterbury-Stowe Road toward US-2/Waterbury. At the traffic circle, take the third exit onto North Main Street/US-2E. After 1.3 miles, turn right onto VT-100 South. Continue for 7 miles and then turn right to stay on VT-100 South. After approximately 12 miles, the parking area will be on your right. There is enough room for about 20 vehicles, and there is strictly no parking on the road. If the lot is full, you'll have to come back or wait for someone to leave. GPS: N44 5.6508', W72 51.8382'

THE HIKE

If cliff jumping is your jam, Warren Falls is the place to do it. Not only is there ample opportunity to partake in this activity, it's likely one of the safest places to do it. Don't get me wrong—cliff jumping inherently has its risks. But the pools here are clear and deep so you're able to easily gauge exactly where to jump.

WHY IS THE WATER GREEN?

There's a very simple answer here, but there are also other reasons that water might change color. Changes in water color could be due to algae blooms or suspended sediment in the water. Usually when a river looks milky, silt is suspended in the water and light is reflected off it. But in the case of Warren Falls and many other spots in New England, the waters are crystal-clear and give off an emerald hue simply due to the minerals that are dissolved from the rocks that make up the majority of the river bottom and edges. In northern New England, the parent material is dominated by granite, which consists mostly of quartz, feldspar, and mica.

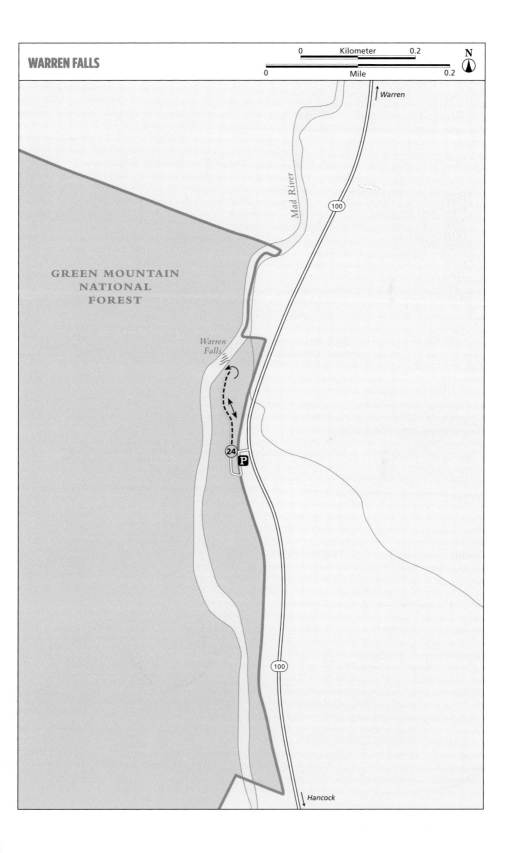

0   Kilometer   0.2

0   Mile   0.2

N

↑ *Warren*

Mad River

100

**GREEN MOUNTAIN
NATIONAL
FOREST**

*Warren
Falls*

24
P

100

↓ *Hancock*

The trail to Warren Falls is quick and easy

The trail opens into otherworldly pools with lots of rock slabs perfect for sunbathing

Take the trail from the parking lot just past the kiosk. There are not a lot of spaces in the parking area, so if it's full, leave and come back another time. The rule about no parking along the roadside is strict—your car will be towed.

The ledges on the far side of the falls have the most sun, so if you're looking to sunbathe, make sure to snag a spot on that side. The huge ledges can hold many visitors, and there's plenty of room for everyone who wants to enjoy the swimming holes.

When I visited, there was a huge log that had fallen and wedged itself between two of the big boulders jutting out of the water. It was fun to watch kids and adults shimmy across the log to jump into the water below.

Make sure to check out all the different pools to see which one might be your favorite. There are several that are shallow enough to be perfect for kids who can't quite swim yet. Once they're able to swim and feeling adventurous, this will still be a great spot to visit.

A log is wedged between two rock slabs, and visitors can jump from it

MILES AND DIRECTIONS

0.00 Start at the northern end of the parking lot past the kiosk.

0.02 Head right down the hill to make your way to the many pools of Warren Falls.

0.12 Reach the base of the river and enjoy the endless pools. When you're done, head back up on the trail.

0.25 Arrive back at the trailhead where your car is parked.

25 **BOLTON POTHOLES**

Another widely popular swimming hole that lives up to its name, Bolton Potholes is one of the most geologically unique spaces in the state. There is something for everyone, including potholes, shallow pools, and waterfalls in one area. Oh, and the view isn't too shabby either.

Start: At the trailhead off Bolton Valley Access Road
Elevation gain: 90 feet
Distance: 0.75 mile out and back
Difficulty: Easy
Hiking time: About 30 minutes
Fees and permits: No fee required
Trail contact: Vermont River Conservancy, 29 Main St., Ste. 11, Montpelier, VT 05602; (802) 229-0820; https://vermontriverconservancy.org
Dog-friendly: Allowed on leash

Trail surface: Granite slabs, dirt, and rocks/roots
Land status: Vermont River Conservancy
Nearest town: Bolton, VT
Other trail users: None
Temperature of water: 65°F
Body of water: Joiner Brook
Water availability: None
Maps: Vermont River Conservancy Bolton Potholes map
Toilets: No
Wheelchair compatibility: No
Family-friendly: Yes

FINDING THE TRAILHEAD
From Burlington, take I-89 South for approximately 10 miles. Take exit 11 for US-2 toward VT-117/Richmond/Bolton. Turn right onto US-2 East and then look for parking off to the left just before the highway underpass. This is the only parking available—there is no parking at the junction or along the edges of Bolton Valley Access Road. This is strictly enforced. Walk to the trailhead along US-2 and then onto Bolton Valley Access Road. This is a very busy road, so please use caution and adhere to pedestrian rules of the road. GPS: N44 22.377', W72 52.806'

THE HIKE
Bolton Potholes has become increasingly more popular over the years, and due to its proximity to privately owned homes, the ways to park there have had to change. But the area still remains free of charge and open to the public.

Start the trek to Bolton Potholes by parking on the northern side of US-2. This is an extremely busy road where the speed limit is 55 mph (although drivers go much faster than that). Please use caution when walking on the side of the road to get to the access road. You'll walk underneath the I-89 underpass and then take a left onto Bolton Valley Access Road. Walk another 0.15 mile and then find the signage for Bolton Potholes.

Head up the small trail that is on the other side of the guardrail to where you reach a fork. You can go right to hike down to the lower parts of the potholes or head straight to get to the area at the top of the falls. Either one is a good option, so it's up to you which way you want to go.

If you stick to the lower end, you'll be greeted with a large swimming hole at the base of the falls. This area is perfect for smaller kids or those who want to wade in slowly. You can also reach an almost perfectly shaped circle pothole if you take the lower trail. This

BOLTON POTHOLES

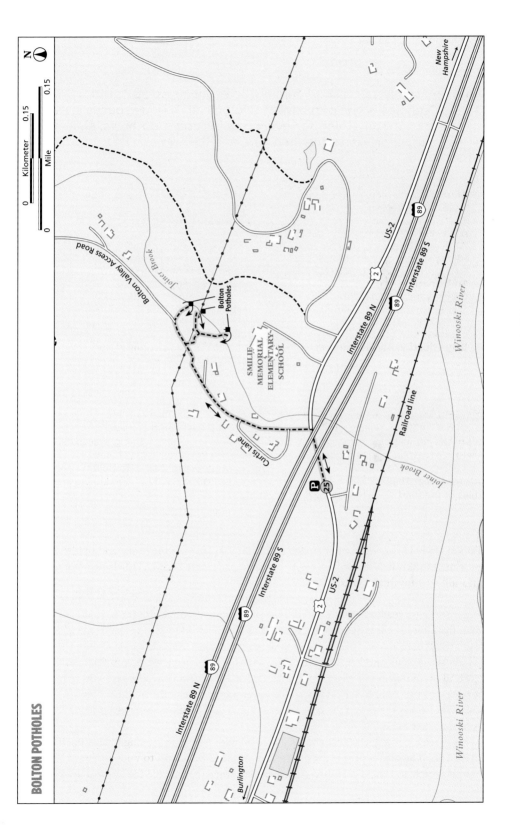

The lowermost
waterfall/pool

A view from the top of the potholes

swimming hole is for anyone who might want to jump in and tread water for a while, since the pool is deeper here.

The pothole just above this one is called "Eagle's Eye" and is where all the drownings have occurred in the area. The whirls that occur within this pothole from the waterfall that descends into it and the current of the waterfall that falls out of it make for a dangerous place to swim. Please refrain from swimming in this particular hole.

If you head up the trail to the upper part of the potholes, there's another great spot for families and others to wade in and dip their toes in the water. There are plenty of slabs for you to stretch out and sunbathe or have a small picnic.

Despite the popularity of this swimming hole, it's surprisingly clean and well looked after. I'm not sure if it's locals who clean up or if visitors just respect this area so much. Even when there are dozens of people here, it's still worth the visit. When you're finished, head back down the trail and onto the access road to get back to your car.

MILES AND DIRECTIONS

0.00   Start at the side of US-2. Head toward the I-89 underpass.

0.05   Go under I-89 and turn left onto Bolton Valley Access Road.

0.20   Take the small trail on the southeastern side of the road; look for a kiosk with information about Bolton Potholes. Take the trail straight to reach the spur trails to the potholes.

0.25   Reach the spur trail for the lower end of the potholes. Make your way down and try out those swimming holes before heading back to the main trail and ascending to the upper part.

0.40   Get back on the main trail and take a right.

0.45   Reach the upper end of Bolton Potholes.

0.55   Intersect with Bolton Valley Access Road yet again and walk down toward US-2.

The trail to Bolton Potholes hugs the road closely

0.70 Take a right onto US-2. Again, be aware of your surroundings and take care while walking along the road.

0.75 Arrive back at your car parked alongside the road.

GEOLOGY OF POTHOLES

When geologists talk about potholes, they are not talking about the things in the road that pop your tires. Instead, they're speaking about a much more scientific type of geological formation found all over the world. A pothole is any smooth, cylindrical hole that is usually deeper than it is wide. They will always occur along a waterway and are some of the most unique geological formations in the country. Potholes were formed thousands of years ago during the last ice age when the glaciers started to retreat. The sediment they were carrying would carve out large holes that would slowly swirl more and more sediment around, creating a funnel deeper down into the ground.

26 BINGHAM FALLS

Hands down, Bingham Falls is the most spectacular geologic site in Smugglers' Notch State Park. Luckily for you, it's also a swimming hole for those brave enough to risk the chilly waters. The roaring waterfall acts as a beautiful background for your swimming adventure. Surrounded by huge boulders, this majestic pool is truly a remarkable sight.

Start: At the Bingham Falls trailhead
Elevation gain: 20 feet
Distance: 0.5 mile out and back
Difficulty: Easy to moderate (due to elevation loss/gain)
Hiking time: About 30 minutes
Fees and permits: No fee required
Trail contact: Vermont State Parks, 1 National Life Dr., Davis 2, Montpelier, VT 05620; (888) 409-7579; https://vtstateparks.com/smugglers.html
Dog-friendly: Allowed on leash
Trail surface: Dirt, rocks/roots, and stone stairs

Land status: US Forest Service
Nearest town: Stowe, VT
Other trail users: None
Temperature of water: 60°F
Body of water: West Branch Little River
Water availability: None
Maps: Smugglers' Notch State Park trail map
Toilets: No
Wheelchair compatibility: No
Family-friendly: No

FINDING THE TRAILHEAD

From Stowe, head north on VT-108/Mountain Road for approximately 6.4 miles. Just after signs for the Stowe Scenic Auto Road, the large parking lot will be on your right. Overflow parking is also available on the opposite side of the road. GPS: N44 31.0908', W72 46.1724'

THE HIKE

Heading north from Stowe to get to Smugglers' Notch State Park is a joy in and of itself. Before you go to Bingham Falls, make sure to head all the way up VT-108 to drive the winding road to Smugglers' Notch Visitor Center. Learn about the history of the area and how it got the name "Smugglers' Notch." (Spoiler—you can check out why in the sidebar.)

Return to the parking area on the east side of VT-108. From the parking lot, the main trail is easy to see next to the kiosks. Here you'll learn about William Bingham, for whom the waterfall is named. He's well known in these parts as the man who convinced the town of Stowe to build a toll road up Mount Mansfield, where he built the Notch House. Early photographs of Bingham Falls describe the falls as Orpha Cascade—Orpha being the name of Bingham's wife. Most people like to think that Bingham Falls is named for the two of them.

When you hit the edge of the gorge, take a look down into the ravine. You'll see rock carved by thousands of years of powerful water hitting its surfaces. This area is gorgeous but also very dangerous to swim in. Do not attempt to jump into any of the pools above Bingham Falls.

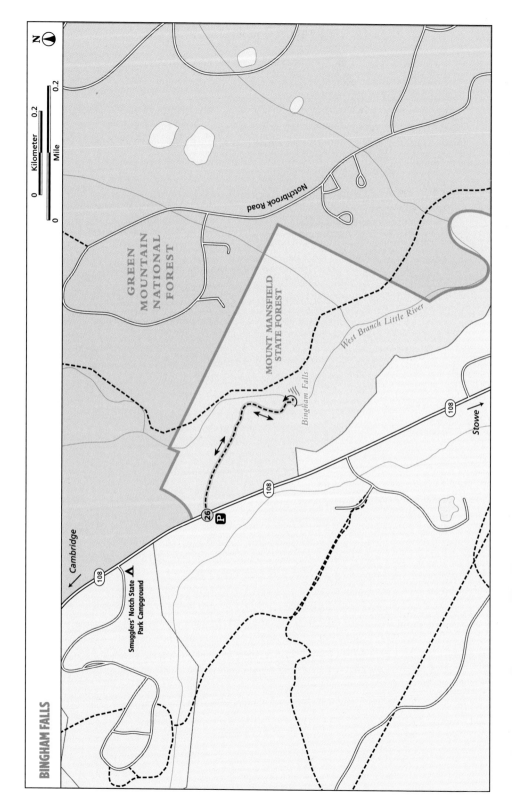

BINGHAM FALLS

GREEN MOUNTAIN NATIONAL FOREST

MOUNT MANSFIELD STATE FOREST

Notchbrook Road

West Branch Little River

Bingham Falls

Cambridge

Smugglers' Notch State Park Campground

Stowe

N

0   Kilometer   0.2

0   Mile   0.2

At just under 0.2 mile, turn right to head down to the base of the falls. Not long after, you'll hit a sign that says "View of Falls, Steep Trail Down"—and the sign is not lying. It's very steep and potentially slippery, even when rain hasn't occurred recently. Please use caution when descending the steps, and if you are at all unsure of your feet, do not attempt to hike down.

You'll arrive at the base of the falls 0.25 mile from the start of the trail. There is a huge rock slab where you can view the falls and hang out for a bit. I did this as I watched some visitors swim in the pool at the base of Bingham Falls. Large boulders flank the pool around the falls and are enticing to jump from. However, management requests that people refrain from jumping for safety precautions.

Soak in the cooling waters below the massive waterfall until you can't feel your toes. On second thought, maybe get out before you lose feeling in your toes. Then make your way back up the steep stone steps and head left when you reach the top to return to the trailhead.

MILES AND DIRECTIONS

0.00 Start at the Bingham Fall trailhead on the eastern side of VT-108.

0.18 Turn right to descend to the base of the falls.

The view from upstream of Bingham Falls—do NOT attempt to swim here

Bingham Falls in the early morning light

Tread carefully; the trail to the river is very steep and frequently slippery

0.22 Begin the steep descent along stone steps toward Bingham Falls.

0.25 Reach the base of the falls. After swimming in the pool, head back up the steep incline to get back to your car.

0.32 Take a left to continue toward the parking lot.

0.50 Arrive back at the trailhead.

A SITE EXPLODING WITH ILLEGAL ACTIVITY

Smugglers' Notch State Park has a shady history. Back in the early 1800s, President Thomas Jefferson put forth the Embargo Act of 1807, which ultimately forbade trade with Britain and its territories. Vermonters depended heavily on trade with Canada, which was (and is still part of the Commonwealth) a territory of Britain at the time.

The Embargo Act forced their hand to start smuggling goods and herding cattle across the mountain pass that is now called Smugglers' Notch. The difficult terrain and assortment of caves in the area made it easy for tradesmen to smuggle things across the border. Even fugitive slaves used this route to make their way to freedom in Canada. The route was eventually improved to allow cars to pass through, which helped greatly during Prohibition, when alcohol became illegal. The caves were used to store the alcohol waiting to cross the border when it was safe to do so. Today, Smugglers' Notch is home to hikers and outdoor enthusiasts.

27 TERRILL GORGE

Terrill Gorge is one of those lesser-known swimming holes, so you'll likely have the place to yourself. There isn't a trail to get you there; instead, you'll have to ford the river to get to the swimming hole. The effort is well worth it, though, when you see the magical pool underneath the 10-foot-wide waterfall.

Start: Off Stagecoach Road
Elevation gain: 140 feet
Distance: 0.8 mile out and back
Difficulty: Easy to moderate (due to scrambling)
Hiking time: About 30 minutes
Fees and permits: No fee required
Trail contact: Green Mountain & Finger Lakes National Forests, PO Box 220, Rutland, VT; (802) 747-6700; www.fs.usda.gov/recarea/gmfl
Dog-friendly: Allowed on leash

Trail surface: Wading the river, dirt, and rocks/roots
Land status: US Forest Service
Nearest town: Stowe, VT
Other trail users: None
Temperature of water: 65°F
Body of water: Kenfield Brook
Water availability: None
Maps: Green Mountain National Forest map
Toilets: No
Wheelchair compatibility: No
Family-friendly: No

FINDING THE TRAILHEAD
From Stowe, head north on VT-100 for approximately 1.6 miles. Take a slight left onto Stagecoach Road and travel for an additional 6.5 miles. The small dirt parking lot will be on your left. It looks just like a pullout right at the edge of the forest. There is enough parking for a few cars. GPS: N44 34.1688', W72 37.0578'

THE HIKE
There are no signs indicating that you've parked in the correct spot for Terrill Gorge. If you put it into your GPS system, it'll likely take you farther up VT-100 and down a different road. This is not the correct spot, so do not rely on your personal GPS to get you there. The parking area is a pullout on the side of VT-100 at the edge of a forested area before the land opens to houses and private property.

From your vehicle, head through the small bushes and into the trees. It might seem like you've got the wrong place but, believe me, you're on the correct trail. Once you get through the bushes, you'll see an obvious trail in front of you descending to the river valley below. There are several social trails that go off in all different directions from this main trail; do not take them. They are likely from the surrounding private properties and should not be used by the public.

The wide trail leads down to the water's edge, where it will seem like the trail has ended. Technically it has, and you'll wade in the river here. Bring good water shoes, or take off your sneakers/boots so you can keep them dry.

There are two ways to get to the pool at the bottom of the falls along Terrill Gorge. One way is to cross the river to the other side and follow the obvious trail on the west side. This brings you through a small field and then up a steep section to get a nice view

TERRILL GORGE

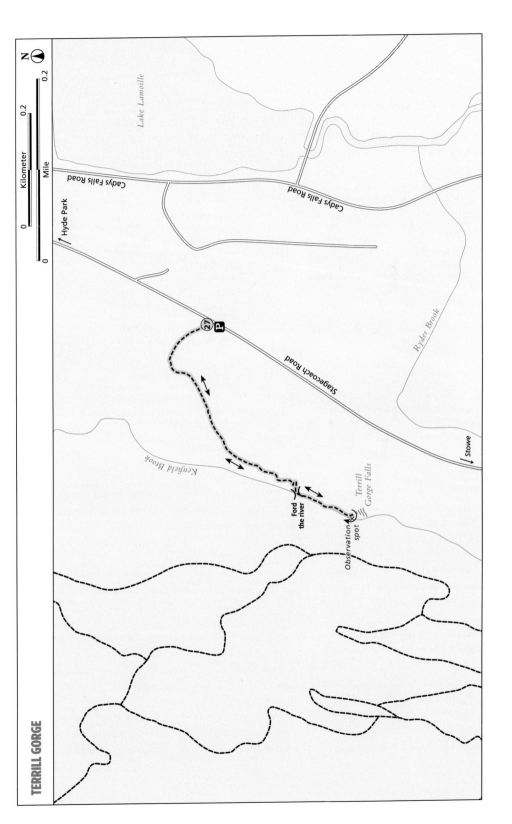

N

Kilometer
0   0.2   0.2

Mile
0   0.2

Lake Lamoille

Cadys Falls Road

Cadys Falls Road

Hyde Park

27 P

Stagecoach Road

Ryder Brook

Stowe

Kenfield Brook

Ford
the river

Terrill
Gorge Falls

Observation
spot

The trail isn't easily seen from the road but opens up once you get past the pullout

THE FAIRY TALE OF HOW TREES RECEIVED THEIR PINECONES

During my college years, I had a great dendrology (study of trees) professor who told us about the pinecone fairy. You see, way back when the world was created, there was a pinecone fairy. All the pines, hemlocks, cedars, larches, and more lined up to see the pinecone fairy to receive their unique pinecone size and characteristics. The sugar pine was first in line and was given the largest pinecone on the planet. Their pinecones can grow up to 2 feet long! The sugar pine was so proud, and they stand tall (and are the tallest pine in the world) to this day.

As the pinecone fairy went through the line, they gave out all the pinecones they had in their arsenal. Some tree species, like the jack pine, annoyed the pinecone fairy and were given cones that only release their seeds with high heat (scientists call these cones "serotinous"). The Douglas firs were a bit scared of the pinecone fairy, so they were given unique cones that looked as if a mouse was hiding under each of the scales of the cone.

But the poor eastern hemlock was last in line. As the pinecone fairy dug through what they had left, there was only one cone. It was the smallest of cones and given to the eastern hemlock. The eastern hemlock felt ashamed by how tiny its cone was compared to the others. And to this day, the eastern hemlock hangs its head in shame. You can always recognize an eastern hemlock from far away if the top of the tree hangs limply to one side.

of the falls. For those not wanting to swim, this is a good option. If you are here to swim, though, you'll go a different way.

Instead of crossing the river, wade in and follow the river upstream. Do not try to walk on the banks of the river, as they are easily eroded and damaged. There are a few spots where you'll have to rock-hop before getting back into the water. Luckily, the pool at the bottom of the falls isn't very far up the river, and you'll be there before you know it. Once you reach the area, there's a small gravel "beach" to your left where you can lay out your clothes and towel. Bring a dry bag to carry your clothes and towel in, since your bag will get wet on your way to the falls.

Then relax and float in the large pool for however long you like. The area is completely forested, so the water tends to be a bit cooler than other swimming holes in the area. When it's a hot and humid day in New England, though, frigid water is welcome. Once you've finished floating and swimming in this peaceful pool, head back down the river. You'll see the trail off to your right, where you'll get back on dry land. Change into dry clothes and boots and take the wide trail back up to the small parking area.

The trail brings you to the water, then you ford the river to get to the swimming hole

Swimming at the base of the falls will feel like a fairy tale

MILES AND DIRECTIONS

0.00 Start on the western side of Stagecoach Road. The trail goes in through some small bushes and then opens into the forest.

0.10 Turn left to head down toward the river's edge.

0.25 Ford the river to lessen the impacts on the surrounding banks.

0.40 Reach the swimming hole at the bottom of the falls at Terrill Gorge. Go back the way you came when you're finished.

0.55 Get back on dry land and turn right to head back up the trail.

0.70 Turn right to steeply climb out of the valley and back to the small parking area.

0.80 Arrive back at your car.

NEW HAMPSHIRE

A gorgeous sunrise over Mountain Pond

28 PACKERS FALLS

This well-known local favorite sits quietly in between the bustling university town of Durham and the quaint village of Newmarket, New Hampshire. And due to its location, you should expect to see a lot of college-aged kids in the area. But don't let that deter you from this swimming hole that is sure to keep you cool on a humid New England day.

Start: Off Bennett Road
Elevation gain: 30 feet
Distance: 0.1 mile out and back
Difficulty: Easy
Hiking time: About 5 minutes
Fees and permits: No fee required
Trail contact: Lamprey River Advisory Committee, c/o 88 Hedding Rd., Epping, NH 03042; www.lampreyriver.org; and Packers Falls Park, 8 Newmarket Rd., Durham, NH 03824; (603) 868-5571; www.ci.durham.nh.us/boc_conservation/packers-falls-park

Dog-friendly: Allowed on leash
Trail surface: Dirt and rocks
Land status: Lamprey River Advisory Committee and Town of Durham
Nearest town: Newmarket, NH
Other trail users: None
Temperature of water: 65°F
Body of water: Lamprey River
Water availability: None
Maps: Packers Falls Road Access nature reserve map
Toilets: No
Wheelchair compatibility: No
Family-friendly: Yes

FINDING THE TRAILHEAD

From Portsmouth, take NH-16 North/US-4 West/Spaulding Turnpike heading toward Concord/Rochester. After 4.7 miles, use the right 2 lanes to exit toward US-4 West. Take a left onto US-4 West and continue for 0.3 mile. At the traffic circle, take the second exit to stay on US-4 West. Travel for approximately 3.4 miles and take the NH-108 exit toward Durham/Dover. Turn left onto NH-108 South for 0.7 mile. Turn left to stay on NH-108 South for 1.5 miles, then turn right onto Bennett Road. Drive for approximately 1.6 miles. The parking area will be on your left just before the intersection of Packers Falls Road. There is enough room for 4 cars. GPS: N43 6.2364', W70 57.0978'

THE HIKE

Like many other swimming holes in this guide, there isn't much of a hike down to the base of Packers Falls. It's more like a small trail from the parking lot to get to the right spot. There are multiple social trails that go down to the bank, but use the largest and most obvious one to prevent further damage to the area.

The falls are only a few hundred feet from the parking lot. There are lots of areas to spread out along the many rock slabs that flank the river. The bank is quite shaded by the surrounding trees on the northern side of the river. If you cross the bridge and go down the southern side, there is a big slab of rock ideal for laying out a towel and sunbathing.

Feel free to bring tubes to float down the river, although make sure not to go too far, as it would be a haul to get back up the river. This area is also popular for fishing, although you likely won't see many anglers during the day in the summer, since swimmers scare away all the fish.

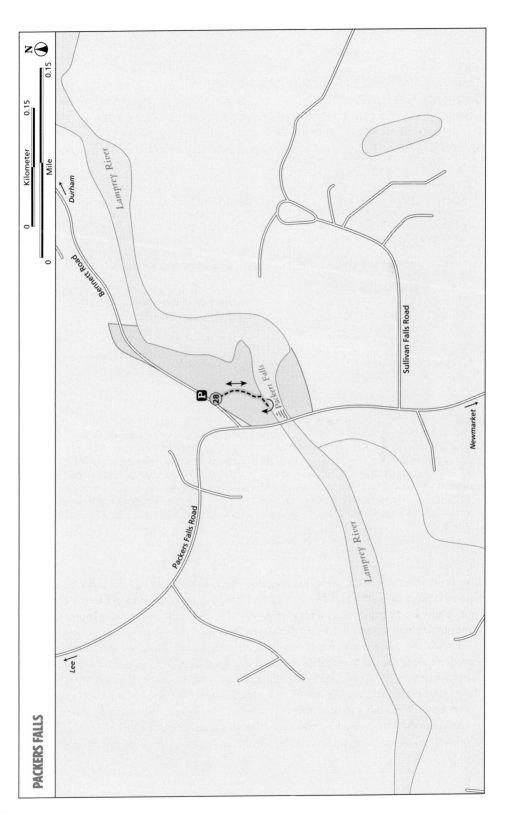

PACKERS FALLS

A view of the bridge across the Lamprey River

THE MILLING INDUSTRY OF THE LAMPREY

The Lamprey River Advisory Committee is committed to preserving the history and integrity of the Lamprey River. As such, they've done extensive research on the history of the river and found there were once over a hundred mills within the watershed. Most of the mills were sawmills or gristmills that were usually family-run and not commercially managed.

One of the more famous mills was the mill complex at Wiswall's Falls in Durham. Brothers Moses and Issachar Wiggin engineered this mill with turbines to more efficiently capture the flow of water. Products from their mill included lumber, pitchforks, knives, flour, axe handles, sleighs, and even matches. Eventually, they added a paper mill to manufacture wallpaper on-site as well. Ironically, as with many paper mills in the nation, the buildings succumbed to a fire in 1883. Finally, a flood in 1896 destroyed the rest of the buildings in the complex.

The Lamprey River is part of the Wild and Scenic River System. This was an act created by Congress back in 1968 to protect and preserve rivers across the nation that provided natural, cultural, and recreational values. The Lamprey River is rife with historical and cultural significance during the time of the milling industry. As you will soon discover, it also has numerous recreational activities along its length.

MILES AND DIRECTIONS

0.00 Start from the parking area off Bennett Road.

0.05 Arrive at the base of Packers Falls. Go back the way you came.

0.10 Arrive back at the trailhead.

The trail to the falls is lined with hardwood trees

29 SOUHEGAN RIVER

As a tributary to the Merrimack River, the Souhegan River is a calm flow that allows recreationists the opportunity to relax in its waters without having to race against a current. The lack of shade surrounding the swimming hole also warms up the waters compared to other rivers in the area. Don't worry, it'll still cool you down.

Start: At the small parking lot off Boston Post Road
Elevation gain: 5 feet
Distance: 0.2 mile out and back
Difficulty: Easy
Hiking time: About 5 minutes
Fees and permits: No fee required
Trail contact: NH Department of Environmental Services, 29 Hazen Dr., Concord, NH 03302; (800) 735-2964; www.des.nh.gov/water/rivers-and-lakes/rivers-management-and-protection
Dog-friendly: Allowed on leash

Trail surface: Sand and dirt
Land status: New Hampshire Department of Environmental Services
Nearest town: Merrimack, NH
Other trail users: None
Temperature of water: 70°F
Body of water: Souhegan River
Water availability: None
Maps: Merrimack road map
Toilets: No
Wheelchair compatibility: No
Family-friendly: Yes

FINDING THE TRAILHEAD

From Manchester, take I-293 South for approximately 3 miles. Keep left at the fork to continue on Everett Turnpike, following signs for Manchester/Merrimack/Nashua. Travel for 8.5 miles and then take exit 11 toward US-3/Merrimack. Turn right onto Camp Sargent Road and continue onto Amherst Road. Drive for approximately 4.5 miles and turn left onto Thornton Ferry Road II. Travel for 1.2 miles before turning left onto Boston Post Road. The small parking area will be 0.2 mile down the road on the left-hand side. The parking lot can fit about 10 cars. GPS: N42 49.6284', W71 35.094'

THE HIKE

The Souhegan River swimming hole is great for families and those wanting calm waters to swim in. The river has a low grade, which means that the river bottom is sandier and siltier compared to other rivers that are fast moving.

Make your way from the parking lot to the small trail on its northeastern side to get down to the river. In a few hundred feet, you'll see the river on your left with a set of stairs that descend into the water. I suggest heading a bit farther on the sandy trail into the shade to set up your blanket and towel for the day.

Farther down the trail, there's a rope swing that looks a little worn. I'm not sure I'd trust it to hold any weight, but I did see a few kids use it and they seemed fine. Use it at your own risk, then, I suppose. For more fun, bring a floating device like many other visitors do. This section of the river is ideal for it since the waters are so calm and lovely to float on and soak in the sun.

The river bends to the southeast at the tree with the rope swing. The water gets a tad shallower around the bend as well, but it's still deep enough to jump in. There is no risk

SOUHEGAN RIVER

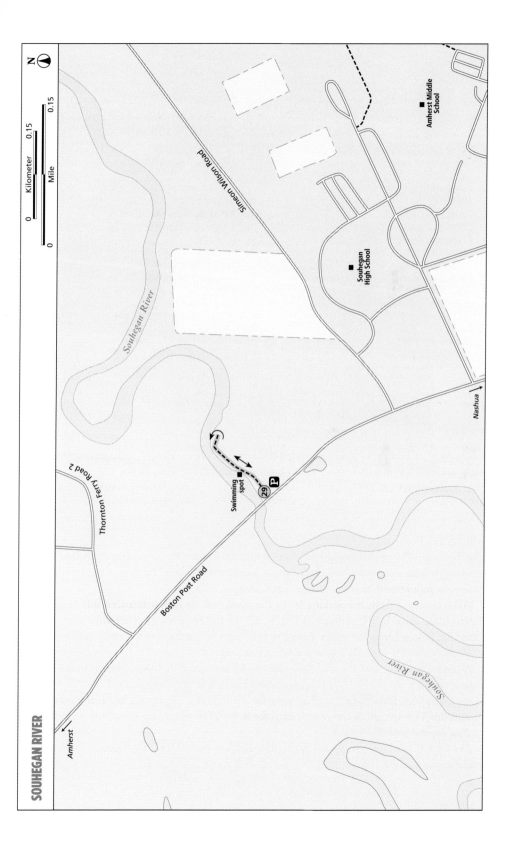

N

Kilometer
0   0.15   0.15

Mile
0   0.15

Souhegan River

Simeon Wilson Road

Amherst Middle School

Souhegan High School

Thornton Ferry Road 2

Boston Post Road

Swimming spot

29

P

Souhegan River

Souhegan River

Amherst

Nashua

You'll find rope swings near the river's edge

of big rocks or boulders on the bottom of this section of river. You can tell what the bottom will feel like since the trails around the swimming hole are mostly sand.

MILES AND DIRECTIONS

- 0.00 Start from the parking area off Boston Post Road.
- 0.05 Reach the river. Head down the trail for a bit more solitude.
- 0.10 Arrive at a glorious swimming hole along the Souhegan River. Turn around and return the same way.
- 0.20 Arrive back at the small parking lot.

WHY ARE SOME RIVERS ROCKY AND OTHERS SANDY?
The makeup of riverbeds largely depends on how powerful the current is in the water and the parent material (i.e., bedrock) underneath the river bottom. Those rivers that have a powerful flow tend to push fine and medium sediment down the river to wherever it eventually flows out. This is why river deltas end up having a siltier texture. What is left behind are gravel, cobblestones, and boulders. On the other hand, those rivers that don't have quite as strong a current tend to have a more sandy, silty river bottom. With less current, the sediment in the river can settle on the bottom instead of getting carried downstream.

30 GILSUM STONE ARCH POOL

The marvel of Gilsum Stone Arch Bridge is also one of the best swimming holes in the state. The steep trail down to the river's edge might scare off a few visitors. However, the view from the bank of the river is breathtaking and worth the ache in your thighs as you descend the 65 (almost vertical) feet.

Start: At the small parking lot off Surry Road
Elevation gain: 65 feet
Distance: 0.2 mile out and back
Difficulty: Easy to moderate (due to steepness)
Hiking time: About 10 minutes
Fees and permits: No fee required
Trail contact: NH Department of Environmental Services, 29 Hazen Dr., Concord, NH 03302; (800) 735-2964; www.des.nh.gov/water/rivers -and-lakes/rivers-management-and -protection
Dog-friendly: Not allowed

Trail surface: Dirt, fallen leaves, and rocks/roots
Land status: New Hampshire Department of Environmental Services
Nearest town: Gilsum, NH
Other trail users: None
Temperature of water: 65°F
Body of water: Ashuelot River
Water availability: None
Maps: Gilsum road map
Toilets: No
Wheelchair compatibility: No
Family-friendly: No

FINDING THE TRAILHEAD

From Manchester, take I-93 North for approximately 12 miles. Take the exit onto I-89 North. Drive for approximately 9 miles and then take exit 5 on the left for US-202 West/NH-9 toward Henniker/Keene. Continue on US-9 West for approximately 25.5 miles. Turn right onto NH-123 North for 7.7 miles and then turn left onto Telephone Road for another 0.2 mile. Immediately turn left onto NH-19 South for 6 miles, then turn right onto Surry Road. The small pullout after you cross the bridge will be on your right. GPS: N43 2.3556', W72 16.2186'

THE HIKE

Also known to locals as The Deep Hole, the swimming hole near Gilsum Stone Arch is a real treat for anyone who visits. The Gilsum Stone Arch swimming hole is a natural gorge that was formed thousands of years ago. The giant boulders that border the edges of the Ashuelot River are great for jumping from into the deep pool.

One such boulder is called The Devil's Chair. It is not recommended to climb down (yes, down) onto this boulder. It's easy to drop down onto the big boulder but much more difficult to then climb back up out of it. There have been several rescues here, so avoid it and, instead, stick to the swimming hole.

The trail starts at the small parking area where you head west on Surry Road (away from the bridge). After a few hundred feet, a small trail on your left indicates the path down to the river. This path has no blazes or signs, but you'll know you're on the right trail since you'll descend quickly.

Take every precaution here, especially if you are unsure on your feet. This hike isn't recommended for small children, as the trail to get to the bank is very treacherous.

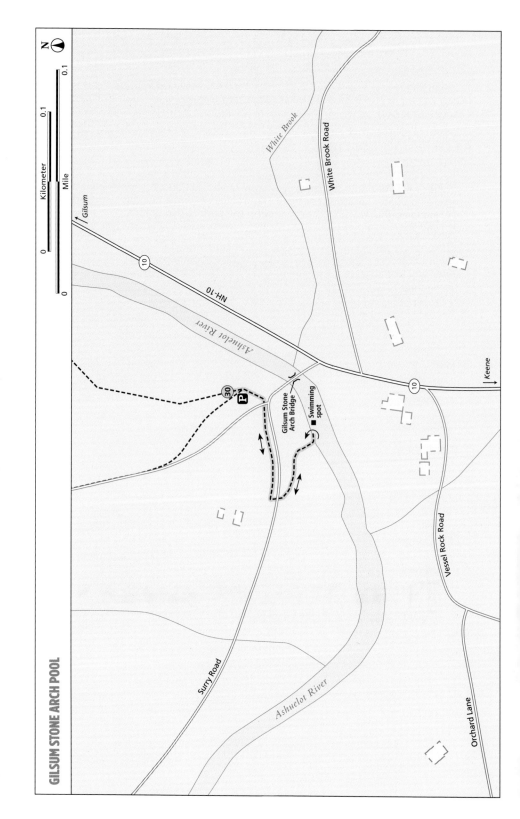

GILSUM STONE ARCH POOL

N

Kilometer
0   0.1

Mile
0   0.1

Gilsum →

10

Ashuelot River

NH-10

White Brook

White Brook Road

Keene →

10

30

P

Gilsum Stone
Arch Bridge

■ Swimming
spot

Surry Road

Ashuelot River

Vessel Rock Road

Orchard Lane

THE TERM "KEYSTONE" ISN'T JUST FOR ARCHES

When architects speak about keystones, they're usually referencing the single stone you place in the middle of an arch that holds the arch together. It's considered the "key" to the arch because if you remove it, the arch collapses. But did you know that biologists also use the term "keystone" but for something that has nothing to do with architecture?

The term "keystone species" refers to a species (plant, animal, or fungal in variety) of such importance in an ecosystem that if it were to die off, the ecosystem would collapse or change drastically. A famous example of this is when wolves were reintroduced into Yellowstone National Park. They were considered a "predator keystone species." The wolves created a healthier ecosystem by changing the way prey moved around the park. When prey moved, the rivers and streams did too. When the water moved, so did other species like bald eagles, bison, and beavers. Reintroducing wolves created a healthier, more dynamic ecosystem where all the flora and fauna thrived.

Other examples of keystone species include sea otters, which keep sea urchins in check among the kelp forests of the oceans, and prairie dogs in the western states, which not only provide a valuable food source for dozens of species but also aerate the soil when they dig their homes.

A beautiful stone arch fills the background of this pool

Be aware of your footfalls when proceeding down the steep path to the river

Looking downstream from the stone arch

Roots and fallen leaves make the trail even more hazardous to walk on, especially if it has recently rained. Once you make it to the bottom, you'll see the swimming hole to your right.

If you look upstream, you can see Gilsum Stone Arch Bridge in all its glory. The bank has a small gravel beach area where you can lay out your belongings. Head downstream to the large boulders that stand high above the swimming hole. You can cross the river to the other side where more rock slabs lie close to the river's edge and are perfect for sunbathing.

When you've had your fill of jumping in the swimming hole, make your way back up the steep trail to head toward the small pullout where you parked your car.

MILES AND DIRECTIONS

0.00   Start from the parking area off Surry Road. Walk west on Surry Road.

0.05   Take a left onto a small trail heading steeply down to the river.

0.10   Arrive at the base of the river with the Stone Arch upstream. Head back up the way you came.

0.15   Turn right onto Surry Road.

0.20   Arrive back at the small parking area.

31 CATAMOUNT POND

There are many New Hampshire state parks that offer nice swimming holes, but Catamount Pond is one of the southernmost ones and has ample recreational activities. There's a small beach with warm waters to swim in, or grab your kayak or SUP to venture farther. Catamount Pond offers a family-friendly spot with barbecues and picnic tables so you can spend your entire day there.

Start: At the parking area at Catamount Pond
Elevation gain: 430 feet
Distance: 2.4 miles out and back
Difficulty: Moderate
Hiking time: About 1 hour
Fees and permits: Fee required
Trail contact: Bear Brook State Park, 157 Deerfield Rd., Allenstown, NH 03275; (603) 485-9874; www .nhstateparks.org/find-parks-trails/ bear-brook-state-park
Dog-friendly: Allowed on leash on trails; prohibited on the beach
Trail surface: Dirt and rocks/roots

Land status: New Hampshire State Parks
Nearest town: Allentown, NH
Other trail users: Mountain bikers
Temperature of water: 75°F
Body of water: Catamount Pond on Bear Brook
Water availability: None
Maps: Bear Brook State Park trail map
Toilets: Yes, at the bathhouse near the beach
Wheelchair compatibility: No
Family-friendly: Yes

FINDING THE TRAILHEAD

From Manchester, take US-3 North for approximately 9 miles. Turn right onto NH-28 North/Pinewood Road and drive for another 3 miles. Turn right onto Deerfield Road for just over 1 mile. The large parking area will be on your left. GPS: N43 9.7308', W71 23.3352'

THE HIKE

Bear Brook State Park encompasses more than 10,000 acres and is the largest developed state park in New Hampshire. There are so many things to see and do in the area, and cabins within the park are available to stay overnight. Dozens of trails are found throughout the park, including over 40 miles of hiking paths. Most people who visit the area are only here for the swimming areas, fishing spots, and the campground, so anyone who ventures onto the trails will likely find themselves in solitude.

Start the trail at the parking lot for Catamount Pond. You'll cross over Deerfield Road and turn right to walk a few hundred feet to the trailhead entrance. Start on the One-Mile Trail and head south (there's only one way to go). Around 0.3 mile in, stay right at the fork to get on the Catamount Trail. You'll take this trail the entire way up to Catamount Hill.

Catamount Hill isn't the highest summit in the park, and unfortunately there are no views at the top, as it is completely forested in. However, there is one overlook around the 0.8-mile mark. Many hikers turn around here since there are no more views if you're just doing the out-and-back trail. Keep heading up the trail until you reach a large cairn.

CATAMOUNT POND

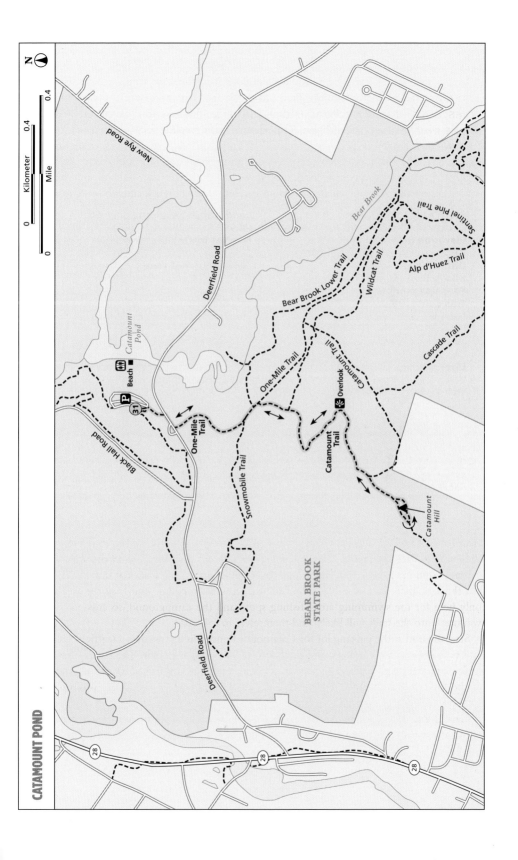

Here you can take the quick walk up to Catamount Hill to say that you summited. Then make your way back down.

When you reach the cairn again, you can continue back the way you came, or you can head right to stay on the Catamount Trail and check out a few more overlooks (although they are about the same as the first overlook). If you go that way, you'll eventually loop back to the One-Mile Trail and head left to return to the trailhead.

Otherwise, continue down Catamount Trail until you reach the first overlook you came across when you ascended. Take a break and allow yourself a moment to savor the views in front of you before continuing down the trail. Veer left when you intersect One-Mile Trail once again. Turn right when you hit Deerfield Road and cross it to head back to the parking lot.

Grab your swim gear, towels, and food and snag one of the picnic tables and barbecues so you can have a cookout after your big hike. There's a bathhouse at the beach where you can change into your swimsuit before diving into the pond. The beach is sandy and ideal for little kids to make sand castles and play while the adults can relax and lounge on their blankets.

A less busy part of the pond for visitors float on the water

A child grabs a shovel to play along the water's edge

MILES AND DIRECTIONS

0.00 Start from the parking area at Catamount Pond.

0.10 Cross Deerfield Road and head right to get to the trailhead for Catamount Hill. Start walking on One-Mile Trail.

0.35 At the fork, veer right onto Catamount Trail.

0.80 Reach an overlook. You can stop here and turn around since there are no more views for the rest of the hike.

1.00 Reach a cairn and fork in the trail. Stay straight to head up to Catamount Hill (no view though), or you can head left and continue on Catamount Trail to do a loop.

1.20 Reach the summit of Catamount Hill.

1.40 Stay straight to head down the way you came, or go right to continue on Catamount Trail and see more views.

1.60 Find your way back to the first overlook and breathe it all in once again.

2.05 Veer left to get back on One-Mile Trail.

2.30 Take a right onto Deerfield Road and cross the street to get back to the parking lot at Catamount Pond.

2.40 Arrive back at the parking lot. Grab your swim gear and head to Catamount Pond for the rest of the day.

32 SCULPTURED ROCKS NATURAL AREA

Enter into a realm that looks as if it were plucked from a fairy tale. The geological formations at Sculptured Rocks Natural Area are unmatched and will leave your jaw agape on the dirt ground. Make sure to close your mouth before you head down to the bank and wade into the crisp, clear river so you don't swallow any water. This place has a different type of magic than any of the other swimming holes in this guide, so make sure to hit this one up.

Start: At the small parking lot off Boston Post Road
Elevation gain: 30 feet
Distance: 0.3 mile out and back
Difficulty: Easy
Hiking time: About 15 minutes
Fees and permits: Fee required
Trail contact: Sculptured Rocks Natural Area, 251 Sculptured Rocks Rd., Hebron, NH 03241; (603) 277-8745; www.nhstateparks.org/find-parks-trails/sculptured-rocks-natural-area
Dog-friendly: Allowed on leash

Trail surface: Dirt and rocks/roots
Land status: New Hampshire State Parks
Nearest town: Hebron, NH
Other trail users: None
Temperature of water: 65°F
Body of water: Cockermouth River
Water availability: None
Maps: Sculptured Rocks Natural Area trail map
Toilets: No
Wheelchair compatibility: No
Family-friendly: Yes

FINDING THE TRAILHEAD

From Concord, take I-93 North for approximately 30 miles. Take exit 23 for NH-104/NH-132 toward Meredith/New Hampton. Keep left at the fork to merge onto NH-104 West/NH-132 South for 1 mile. Continue on NH-104 West for approximately 5 miles and then continue on NH-3A North/Lake Street for another 2 miles. Then turn left onto West Shore Drive for 7.3 miles. Turn left onto Groton Road, which turns into Sculptured Rocks Road after 1.6 miles. Drive for an additional 1.2 miles; parking will be on your left. There are enough spaces for about 30 cars, but this area is very popular, so come early to snag a spot. GPS: N43 42.3912', W71 51.3996'

THE HIKE

Words can't really describe the whimsy and wonder of Sculptured Rocks Natural Area. Thousands of years ago, as the last ice age was wrapping up, this narrow canyon was formed. The sediment that was suspended within the river sanded down, shaped, and smoothed the incredible rock formations you see today.

From the parking area, take the trail that heads into the woods to the right. You'll cross Sculptured Rocks Road, so be sure to take care when walking across. The trail descends to a kiosk where you can pay the fee to get in. There is no host here, so payment is on the honor system. Although many people hike without paying the fee, I implore you to pay the $4 because the money goes directly to managing the area.

Cross the bridge and head right along the path to get to the river's edge. You can choose from several spots in this area, so make sure to explore a bit before deciding where

SCULPTURED ROCKS NATURAL AREA

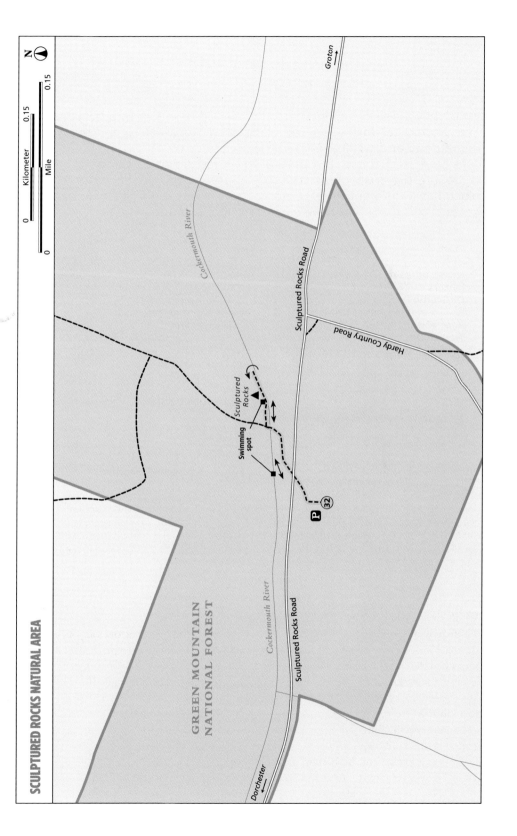

N

Kilometer
0   0.15

Mile
0   0.15

GREEN MOUNTAIN
NATIONAL FOREST

Cockermouth River

Sculptured Rocks Road

Dorchester

Sculptured
Rocks

Swimming
spot

P

32

Sculptured Rocks Road

Hardy Country Road

Groton

Looking down from the bridge through the canyons at Sculptured Rocks Natural Area

to set up your camp for the day. I prefer the spot just downstream of the bridge, since it's perfect for my kiddo.

There are also huge slabs of rock that tower over the gorge and river below. You can jump from these slabs since the water is crystal-clear and deep enough that you shouldn't even come close to hitting the bottom.

Feel free to explore more downstream or upstream of the bridge. This is a very popular spot, but thankfully there are so many options for swimming and wading that you'll feel isolated from any other visitors. I find the farther you go downstream, the fewer people there are—with views almost as beautiful. My kid and I spent hours here just wandering around, looking at all the different pools and wading into the deeper ones. Make sure you carve out (no pun intended) a whole day to spend here since there is so much to see.

HOW EXACTLY DO ROCKS GET SHAPED BY WATER?

In general, rocks along a stream or river tend to be more rounded and smoother. This is due to the fact that moving rivers and streams churn the water around, so the rocks get pummeled by one another, creating a more polished look. On a grander scale, when water moves through a canyon, the sediment and rocks suspended within the water start to scrape against the sides and carve out divots and holes on the canyon's walls. This is why places like Sculptured Rocks Natural Area are so incredible to see. We're able to witness a river that has cut through strong rock to create these magical-looking canyon walls. All due to a moving river with suspended sediment in its waters.

A child making a dam of rocks along the river's edge

A man jumping into the river flowing through the cliffs

More swimming holes can be found downriver of the sculptured rocks

MILES AND DIRECTIONS

0.00 Start from the Sculptured Rocks Natural Area parking lot.

0.05 Cross the road to get down to the natural area.

0.10 Take a right after crossing over the bridge.

0.15 Arrive at the river's edge and enjoy your time.

0.20 Take a left to head back over the bridge toward the road.

0.25 Cross the road to return to the parking area.

0.30 Arrive back at your car.

33 SMARTS BROOK

Tucked away in a hemlock and hardwood forest lies the pool along Smarts Brook in White Mountain National Forest. This gentle trail guides visitors to a large pool at the base of some small waterfalls. This hike and area is perfect for families or for those wanting to have a mini adventure to an idyllic swimming hole in the wilderness.

Start: At the Smarts Brook trailhead
Elevation gain: 260 feet
Distance: 2.2 miles out and back
Difficulty: Moderate
Hiking time: About 1 hour
Fees and permits: No fee required
Trail contact: White Mountain National Forest, 71 White Mountain Dr., Campton, NH 03223; (603) 536-6100; www.fs.usda.gov/recarea/whitemountain/recarea/?recid=74721
Dog-friendly: Allowed on leash

Trail surface: Dirt and rocks/roots
Land status: US Forest Service
Nearest town: Thornton, NH
Other trail users: None
Temperature of water: 60°F
Body of water: Smarts Brook
Water availability: None
Maps: White Mountain National Forest map
Toilets: No
Wheelchair compatibility: No
Family-friendly: Yes

FINDING THE TRAILHEAD

From Concord, take I-93 North for approximately 48 miles. Take exit 28 for NH-49 toward NH-175/Campton/Waterville Valley. Keep right at the fork to merge onto NH-49 East. Travel for about 5 miles and then turn right into the large parking lot. GPS: N43 53.5116′, W71 34.4706′

THE HIKE

The trail starts at the Smarts Brook trailhead just off NH-49. Do not take the Pine Flats Trail, which is on the eastern side of the parking lot (where it is most obvious to have a trail). Instead, walk south with the road to your right and you'll see another trail. This is the one you want. Walk a few feet south before turning left into the trees. You'll be on the right-hand side of the brook, although you won't see it along this trail for a little while.

Smarts Brook Trail will meet up with an old road that you'll walk on for about 0.2 mile before veering right to continue on the Smarts Brook Trail (yellow blazes). Stay straight at the next intersection when you reach the Tri-Town Trail. Continue straight for the next 0.5 mile or so, where you finally get your first glimpse of Smarts Brook.

Continue another 0.3 mile until you get a really good view of the brook and the small falls that feed into the pool you'll swim in. Depending on the season, the waterfalls might just be trickling over the edge or pouring over the wide slabs. It's rare for this part of the brook to get too out of hand, so you should be all right even when the water is flowing a bit faster than usual.

The nature of the falls allows for the water to fall more evenly and widely over the granite slabs. This spreads out the force of the water so that it isn't plummeting into the pool below. The pool is fairly deep (around 10 feet) and can fit dozens of people if need be.

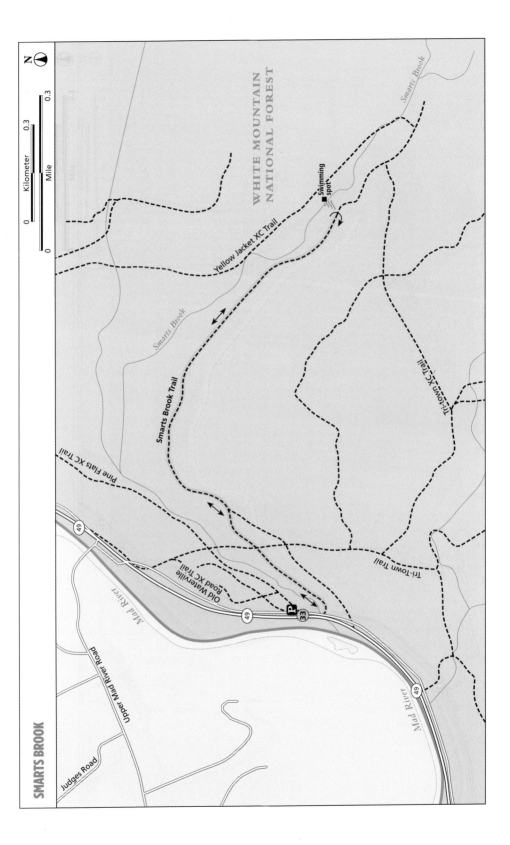

SMARTS BROOK

WHITE MOUNTAIN
NATIONAL FOREST

N

Kilometer
0   0.3   0.3
0   Mile

Mile

Smarts Brook

Yellow Jacket XC Trail

Swimming
spot

Smarts Brook Trail

Smarts Brook

Tri-town XC Trail

Pine Flats XC Trail

Tri-town Trail

Old Waterville
Road XC Trail

P 33

49

49

Mad River

Upper Mad River Road

Judges Road

Mad River

49

Smarts Brook is filled with boulders and small pools all along the river

TRAIL MAGIC

Trail magic is not when a magician in a top hat with a wand shows up on the trail and does a show for you. Instead, trail magic is what is known to thru-hikers as something you find along the trail when you need it the most. This might be finding the perfect campsite after a long day of hiking. It might be watching the most unique cloud formation over a stunning sunset in the middle of the White Mountains. But it can also be purposeful for those of us who aren't thru-hikers. What that means is you can be part of trail magic without having to walk thousands of miles.

I do a bit of trail magic every year, and Smarts Brook is one of the best places to set up shop. I try to do it on a day when rain is forecasted and pack up my car with hot coffee, cocoa, tea, donuts, and some full-size candy bars. Then I head up to a section of the Appalachian Trail with a large canopy, a few camping chairs, and a table to set up all the goodies.

Make sure to time it right, since most thru-hikers will make it to New England later in the summer if they're starting in Georgia. Aim for setting up some trail magic in August if you're in the northern New England states. I also try to do it on a weekday when the parking lots aren't as crowded with day hikers so I'm not in anyone's way.

I will tell you that conducting a little trail magic for AT thru-hikers is one of the most memorable experiences I've ever had. I take my kiddo with me now so he understands how giving back can make you feel really good. And on those rainy days, thru-hikers are so appreciative of the small things that strangers do. So try it; I dare you!

Further upstream along
the trail brings you to
cliffs and deeper pools

A pool along Smarts Brook

Gather your belongings after you've swum your heart out and head back down the trail. The pool is only 1.1 miles from the trailhead, so it should be a quick jaunt back to your car. Make sure to stay on Smarts Brook Trail—don't take any of the trails that branch off it—to make it back to the parking area.

MILES AND DIRECTIONS

0.00   Start at the Smarts Brook trailhead (not the Pine Flats trailhead).

0.05   Turn left into the woods to continue on the trail.

0.20   Cross over the Tri-Town Trail and continue straight.

0.80   Get your first glimpse of Smarts Brook.

1.10   Arrive at the swimming hole, on your left.

1.40   Say good-bye to Smarts Brook as you leave the area.

2.00   Cross back over the Tri-Town Trail.

2.15   Take a right to head north toward the parking lot.

2.20   Arrive back at the trailhead.

34 SWIFTWATER FALLS

There are sixty covered bridges in New Hampshire, but none have as beautiful a swimming hole as Swiftwater Covered Bridge. This gorgeous backdrop to the mesmerizing falls that drop into a gloriously huge pool will keep you coming back year after year.

Start: At the parking lot off Porter Road
Elevation gain: 30 feet
Distance: 0.2 mile out and back
Difficulty: Easy
Hiking time: About 5 minutes
Fees and permits: No fee required
Trail contact: NH Department of Environmental Services, 29 Hazen Dr., Concord, NH 03302; (800) 735-2964; www.des.nh.gov/water/rivers-and-lakes/rivers-management-and-protection
Dog-friendly: Allowed on leash

Trail surface: Sand, dirt, and rock slabs
Land status: New Hampshire Department of Environmental Services
Nearest town: Benton, NH
Other trail users: None
Temperature of water: 65°F
Body of water: Wild Ammonoosuc River
Water availability: None
Maps: Benton road map
Toilets: No
Wheelchair compatibility: No
Family-friendly: Yes

FINDING THE TRAILHEAD
From Concord, take I-93 North for approximately 62 miles. Take exit 32 for NH-112 toward Lincoln/North Woodstock. Turn right onto NH-112 West and drive for 19 miles. Turn right onto Porter Road. Parking is on the left-hand side after you cross the covered bridge, in a large parking lot. GPS: N44 8.0694', W71 57.075'

THE HIKE
The path is easy and quick to get down to Swiftwater Falls, which reside just downstream of Swiftwater Covered Bridge. Go east through the parking lot until you almost reach Porter Road. You'll see a large gravel path on your right to get down to the water's edge. There are other, smaller trails that also lead directly from the parking lot down to the water farther downstream.

Once you make it down to the rock slabs, take a look around. There are several spots to swim, including just under the covered bridge farther upstream. Or you can head down past Swiftwater Falls to swim in the gigantic pool at its base. Many spots also offer shallower waters so little kids can freely wade in and out without being swept downriver.

As can likely be deduced from its name, the current can be fast and strong in this section of the Wild Ammonoosuc River. Only strong swimmers should wander out into the middle of the river. Even then, always use caution, because the current can come quickly and catch you off guard.

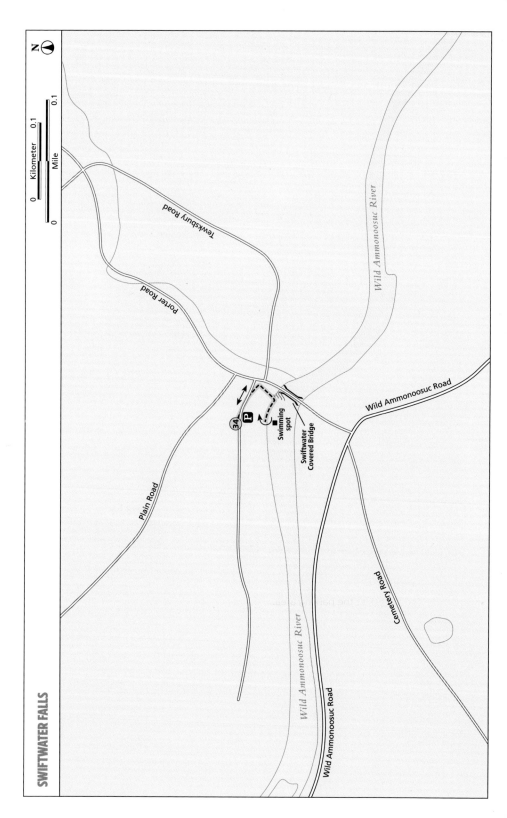

SWIFTWATER FALLS

N

Kilometer
0   0.1
0   0.1
Mile

Plain Road

Porter Road

Tewksbury Road

34

P

Swimming
spot

Swiftwater
Covered Bridge

Wild Ammonoosuc Road

Wild Ammonoosuc River

Wild Ammonoosuc River

Wild Ammonoosuc Road

Cemetery Road

Wild Ammonoosuc River

Swiftwater Covered Bridge crosses the Ammonoosuc River

MILES AND DIRECTIONS

0.00 Start from the parking area off Porter Road.

0.05 Turn right down the gravel path to get to the large slabs along the river.

0.10 Arrive at one of the many huge slabs that border the Wild Ammonoosuc River and the falls that drop downstream of the covered bridge. Feel free to wander and find the best spot to hang out for the day.

0.15 Head back upstream until you reach the gravel path just before the covered bridge. Take a left to return to the parking lot.

0.20 Arrive back at the parking area.

35 LONESOME LAKE

Do you want to eat a big slab of chocolate cake before diving into a wild body of water? Did you think such a thing wasn't possible? It is if you take this trail up to Lonesome Lake! At the summit lies an Appalachian Mountain Club (AMC) hut where the "croo" (aka the staff) whips up some delicious treats for those visiting the area. The trail is short, but the ascent can be brutal. Luckily, the idea of having a sweet treat and resting weary muscles in a cold lake might just entice you to get there quickly.

Start: At the Lonesome Lake trailhead
Elevation gain: 1,025 feet
Distance: 3.1-mile lollipop
Difficulty: Moderate to strenuous (due to steepness)
Hiking time: About 1.5 hours
Fees and permits: No fee required
Trail contact: Franconia Notch State Park, 260 Tramway Dr., Franconia, NH 03580; (603) 823-8800; www .nhstateparks.org/visit/state-parks/ franconia-notch-state-park; and Appalachian Mountain Club, 10 City Square, Boston, MA; (603) 466-2727; www.outdoors.org/destinations/

massachusetts-and-new-hampshire/ zealand-falls-hut
Dog-friendly: Allowed on leash
Trail surface: Dirt and solid rock
Land status: US Forest Service and New Hampshire State Parks
Nearest town: Franconia, NH
Other trail users: None
Temperature of water: 65°F
Body of water: Lonesome Lake
Water availability: At the AMC hut
Maps: White Mountains—Franconia to Pemigewasset trail map
Toilets: Yes, at the AMC hut
Wheelchair compatibility: No
Family-friendly: Yes

FINDING THE TRAILHEAD

From Concord, take I-93 North for approximately 72 miles. Take exit 34B toward Cannon Mountain Tramway. Turn left onto Tramway Drive and make another left to get back on I-93 South for 2.2 miles. Take the exit into Lafayette Place Campground and turn left to the parking lot for Lonesome Lake. GPS: N44 8.5242′, W71 41.0622′

THE HIKE

I've done this hike a bunch of times in the winter because I find the steep trail much easier to navigate that time of year. However, taking a dip in Lonesome Lake when you get to the top is so refreshing, it's worth the huge vert to get there.

The hike starts at the Lonesome Lake trailhead at Lafayette Place Campground. The parking lot is off to the left, although overflow parking can be found on the right. This place can get very busy, and if parking is unavailable, you will have to either wait or come back another time, as there is no parking on the sides of the roads. Head over the small bridge and through the campground to stay on the trail. You will cross some roads within the campground, so use caution with kids when you cross.

This hike is considered moderate to strenuous due to the elevation gain in such a short distance. With that said, even my son (who was 4 years old at the time) made it up to the hut on his own two legs, so it can be done by those who have had a bit more trail experience, even if they are young. There are several places along the steep trail that are

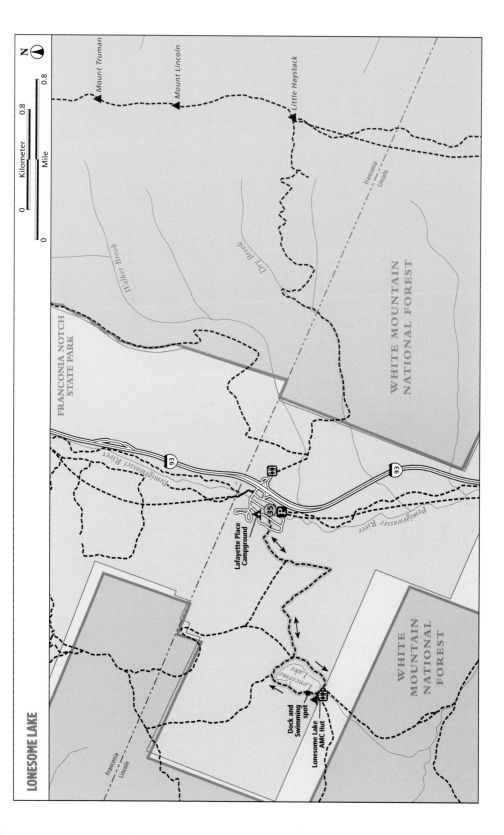

LONESOME LAKE

FRANCONIA NOTCH STATE PARK

WHITE MOUNTAIN NATIONAL FOREST

WHITE MOUNTAIN NATIONAL FOREST

Pemigewasset River

Pemigewasset River

Walker Brook

Dry Brook

Mount Truman

Mount Lincoln

Little Haystack

Franconia
Lincoln

Franconia
Lincoln

Lafayette Place
Campground

Dock and
Swimming
spot

Lonesome Lake
AMC Hut

Lonesome Lake

N

0   Kilometer   0.8

0   Mile   0.8

93

93

35

P

The dock is a great place to keep your towel and gear while you swim

difficult for those with shorter legs to climb. Many times I had to hoist myself up and over tree roots and rocks.

Around the 1.0-mile mark, the trail starts to level off to give you a bit of reprieve before the final push to the lake and hut. In fact, the trail descends slightly right before you reach Lonesome Lake. You arrive at the lake around 1.2 miles. If you look out across the water slightly to your left, you can see the hut tucked in the trees. Turn left when you reach Lonesome Lake to head straight to the hut.

This section of the trail has some raised boardwalks, but they are very rustic, and some are even rotted through. Try to walk on them when you can to help prevent more soil erosion. After 0.25 mile, you will hit the Appalachian Mountain Club's Lonesome Lake Hut. Just like the Zealand Falls Hut, the staff runs the hut all summer long and provides the meals that overnight guests enjoy when staying the night.

You can also buy whatever food they have cooked up that day even if you are just there for a day hike. The few times my son and I have done this trip, there's been potato leek soup, chocolate cake (even gluten free), and muffins for us to purchase. They almost always have hot cocoa, tea, and coffee for those wanting to partake in some caffeine before heading back out on the trail.

A great wooden dock is located down at the lake in front of the hut. From there you can see east to all the 4,000-footers, including Mount Lafayette, Mount Lincoln, and Little Haystack Mountain. The view can truly take your breath away—especially if you have just huffed and puffed your way up the 1,000 feet of vertical elevation gain to get there.

Once you have inhaled the chocolate cake from the hut and feel refreshed, head back around the western side of the lake. The loop will bring you back around to where you first encountered the lake. Turn left to get back on that trail and make your steady descent back to your car. Do not forget that the trail was steep on the way up and can look and feel steeper on the way down. Take as much time as you need to make it back to the trailhead safely.

The trail, like many in New Hampshire, is covered with rocks and roots

MILES AND DIRECTIONS

0.00 Start on the western side of the parking lot.

0.40 Keep straight to stay on the Lonesome Lake Trail. Do not turn right.

1.20 Reach the lake. Turn left to head toward the Lonesome Lake Hut.

1.50 Reach the Lonesome Lake Hut. Continue north on the loop around the lake.

1.90 Meet back up with the Lonesome Lake Trail and retrace your steps back down toward the trailhead.

2.70 Stay straight to head back to your car.

3.10 Arrive back at the trailhead.

36 FRANCONIA FALLS

Thrill-seekers, look no further than Franconia Falls for your next adventure. With natural waterslides, whirling pools, and incredibly strong waterfalls, Franconia Falls fills your adrenaline needs. It might be one of the longer treks to get you to a swimming hole, but the trail is relatively flat and easily done by most skill levels.

Start: At the Lincoln Woods trailhead
Elevation gain: 430 feet
Distance: 6.8 miles out and back
Difficulty: Moderate to strenuous
Hiking time: About 3.5 hours
Fees and permits: Fee required
Trail contact: White Mountain National Forest, 71 White Mountain Dr., Campton, NH 03223; (603) 536-6100; www.fs.usda .gov/recarea/whitemountain/ recarea/?recid=74669
Dog-friendly: Allowed on leash

Trail surface: Dirt and rocks/roots
Land status: US Forest Service
Nearest town: Lincoln, NH
Other trail users: Mountain bikers
Temperature of water: 60°F
Body of water: Franconia Brook
Water availability: At the trailhead
Maps: White Mountain National Forest map
Toilets: Yes, at the trailhead
Wheelchair compatibility: No
Family-friendly: No

FINDING THE TRAILHEAD

From Concord, take I-93 North for approximately 62 miles. Take exit 32 for NH-112 toward Lincoln/North Woodstock. Turn left onto NH-112 East and drive for approximately 5 miles. The Lincoln Woods trailhead entrance will be on your left. This is a huge parking lot but is also quite popular. Depending on the season, the lot could fill up fast. GPS: N44 3.8124', W71 35.2716'

THE HIKE

The Lincoln Woods trailhead is one of the most popular trailheads in the White Mountains (maybe second to Falling Waters, where most do Franconia Ridge from). As such, this area can fill up fast, even as early as 7 a.m. This trailhead services several trails, including many that lead up New Hampshire's famed 4,000-footers.

Start at the Lincoln Woods trailhead, in front and to the left of the ranger station. You'll descend some steps and see a long bridge in front of you that crosses the Pemigewasset River. After the bridge, turn right to head north along the Lincoln Woods Trail. This path is wide and flat, and easily walked by folks of all skill levels.

You'll notice some old railway ties; this area housed flourishing logging camps and 50 miles of railroad tracks during its heyday. Now the area is run by the Forest Service, but you can still see the remnants of the historic logging industry. Make sure you don't take any artifacts that you might find along the trail, as they are protected and should not be removed.

Around 1.4 miles into the hike, you'll meet up with the Osseo Trail. This trail is used by many hikers to ascend several 4,000-footers, including Mount Flume and Mount Liberty. Continue straight on Lincoln Woods Trail. Not much farther after the Osseo Trail junction, you'll reach a damaged bridge that cannot be accessed. You'll either ford the

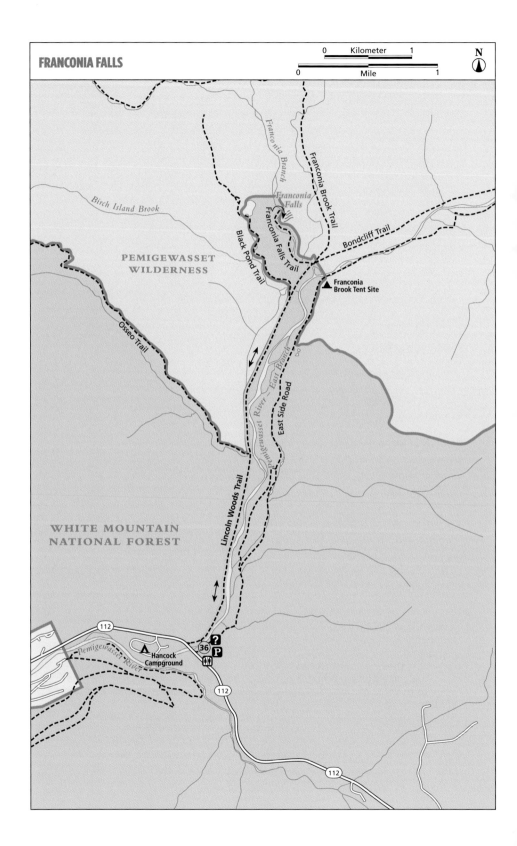

0 Kilometer 1

0 Mile 1

N

Franconia Branch

Franconia Falls

Franconia Brook Trail

Birch Island Brook

Black Pond Trail

Franconia Falls Trail

Bondcliff Trail

PEMIGEWASSET
WILDERNESS

▲ Franconia
Brook Tent Site

Osseo Trail

East Branch

Pemigewasset River

East Side Road

Lincoln Woods Trail

WHITE MOUNTAIN
NATIONAL FOREST

112

⚕ Hancock
Campground

36
P

112

Pemigewasset River

112

112

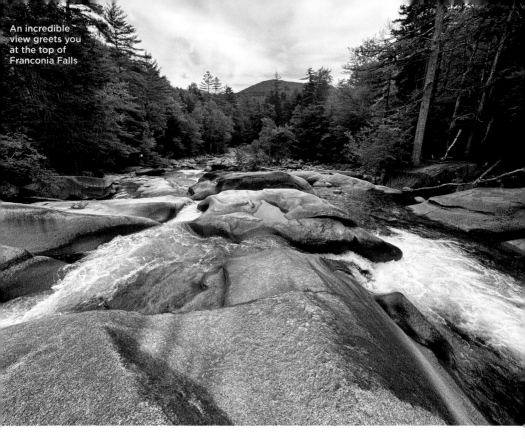

An incredible view greets you at the top of Franconia Falls

small stream or rock-hop to the other side. Depending on the season, this stream could be raging, but it should be fairly easy to cross.

The next thing you'll notice is a trail that goes up to Black Pond on your left. This is a trail that hiking enthusiasts take up to Owl's Head—a rugged 4,000-footer that has no view. Keep going straight until you cross another stream. Shortly after, you'll see the signs for Franconia Falls to the left. This is where you'll gain most of the elevation for the entire trail. At 0.5 mile from the intersection of Lincoln Woods Trail, you'll finally reach Franconia Falls in all its glory.

The falls area can be deadly (and is the site of several fatalities every year), especially during high water. Always check the weather and adhere to any advisories shown on the

WHY ARE THEY CALLED THE WHITE MOUNTAINS?

Just like the Green Mountains, the White Mountains are named for what blankets their summits. No, it's not snow, although in the wintertime you are definitely likely to see a bunch of snow. The White Mountains are called that due to the granite that covers the majority of the higher summits within the national forest. White Mountain National Forest resides mostly in New Hampshire, which is called the Granite State for a reason. The granite that encompasses most of the 4,000-footers and many other trails within the national forest also means that those trails are inherently torturous. For anyone who might be short like I am, your quads will kill you with all the hoisting up boulders you'll be doing on the trails.

kiosks at the beginning of both the Lincoln Woods and Franconia Falls Trails. The falls area is riddled with several flumes—water that quickly and tightly runs through a narrow channel—that are easily jumped over. However, in rainy or dewy conditions, jumping from rock to rock can prove dangerous. There are several pools to swim in at the falls, so take your time to find a good spot. There is even a natural waterslide many use to add some flare to their swim experience.

When you've finished swimming and playing in the falls, head back on Franconia Falls Trail toward Lincoln Woods Trail and turn right. Stay straight on the Lincoln Woods Trail until you once again reach the bridge over the Pemigewasset River. Cross the bridge and make your way back to your car in the parking lot.

MILES AND DIRECTIONS

0.00   Start from the Lincoln Woods trailhead in front and to the left of the ranger station.

0.10   Cross over the bridge to get to the northwestern side of the Pemigewasset River. Turn right to head north.

1.45   Ford/rock-hop the small stream where the bridge is out and cannot be accessed.

1.90   Cross over another small stream.

2.90   Take a left onto Franconia Falls Trail.

For less swift waters, head downstream and wade in the pools further from the falls

There have been several deaths over the years at Franconia Falls due to the slippery rocks and fast-moving water

3.40 Reach Franconia Falls.

3.90 Take a right to get back on Lincoln Woods Trail.

4.90 Cross back over the small stream.

5.35 Ford/rock-hop back over the stream where the bridge is damaged.

6.70 Cross back over the bridge (i.e., turn left) to return to the ranger station.

6.80 Arrive back at the trailhead at the ranger station.

37 THIRTEEN FALLS

Go deep into the wilderness of the White Mountains and swim where very few have swum before. The path to Thirteen Falls is long, but the swimming hole is like no other in this guide. A series of five waterfalls with four glorious pools at their base greet those willing to walk far into the Pemigewasset Wilderness.

Start: At the Lincoln Woods trailhead
Elevation gain: 1,300 feet
Distance: 16.5 miles out and back
Difficulty: Strenuous
Hiking time: About 8 hours
Fees and permits: Fee required
Trail contact: White Mountain National Forest, 71 White Mountain Dr., Campton, NH 03223; (603) 536-6100; www.fs.usda .gov/recarea/whitemountain/ recarea/?recid=74669
Dog-friendly: Allowed on leash
Trail surface: Dirt and rocks/roots

Land status: US Forest Service
Nearest town: Lincoln, NH
Other trail users: Mountain bikers, but none within Pemigewasset Wilderness
Temperature of water: 55°F
Body of water: Franconia Brook
Water availability: Yes, at the trailhead
Maps: White Mountain National Forest map
Toilets: Yes, at the trailhead
Wheelchair compatibility: No
Family-friendly: No

FINDING THE TRAILHEAD

From Concord, take I-93 North for approximately 62 miles. Take exit 32 for NH-112 toward Lincoln/North Woodstock. Turn left onto NH-112 East and drive for approximately 5 miles. The Lincoln Woods trailhead entrance will be on your left. This is a huge parking lot but is also quite popular. Depending on the season, the lot could fill up fast. GPS: N44 3.8124', W71 35.2716'

THE HIKE

The trail to Thirteen Falls initially follows the same trail you take to get to Franconia Falls, so feel free to hit up both in the same day. Start at the Lincoln Woods trailhead in front and to the left of the ranger station. You'll immediately see the large bridge that stretches out over the Pemigewasset River. Turn right after you cross the bridge and head out on the flat trail for about 3 miles.

This is where most visitors turn to head up to Franconia Falls, but you'll continue straight to cross over a smaller bridge that extends over Franconia Brook. Once across the bridge, the trail (now Franconia Brook Trail) heads into the Pemigewasset Wilderness, and you will likely be on your own from here on out.

I'll admit that I got a tad nervous on this trail once I left the popularity of Franconia Falls. The path to Thirteen Falls is as remote as it gets, and it had been awhile since I had truly felt alone out on the trails. This trail harbors the ideal habitat for moose, so in order to make sure I didn't surprise any of them along the way, I ended up singing to myself.

It seemed to do the trick since I didn't get mauled by any wildlife the entire way. Around the 4.5-mile mark you'll reach the intersection with the Lincoln Brook Trail on your left. This is an alternate way to get to Owl's Head—one of New Hampshire's 4,000-footers. Stay straight, though, to continue on Franconia Brook Trail. You'll cross

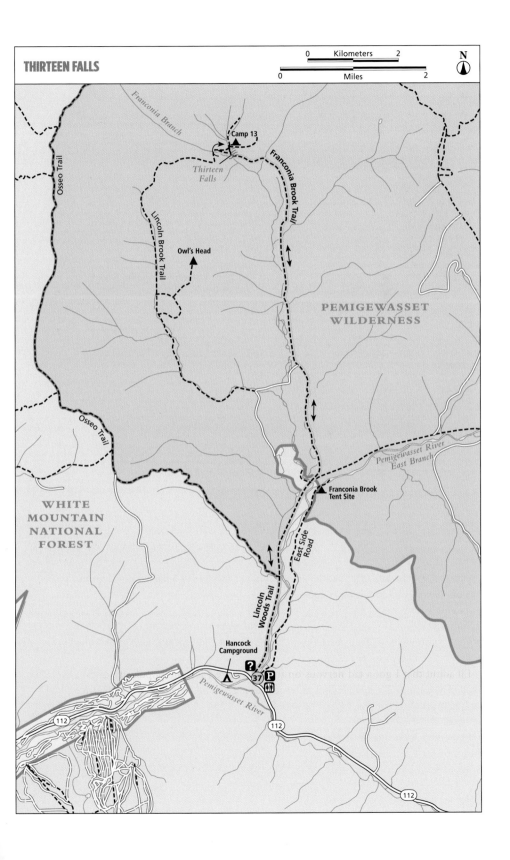

0   Kilometers   2

0   Miles   2

N

Franconia Branch

Osseo Trail

Camp 13

Thirteen Falls

Franconia Brook Trail

Lincoln Brook Trail

Owl's Head

PEMIGEWASSET WILDERNESS

Osseo Trail

Pemigewasset River East Branch

Franconia Brook Tent Site

WHITE MOUNTAIN NATIONAL FOREST

East Side Road

Lincoln Woods Trail

Hancock Campground

37

Pemigewasset River

112

112

112

The well-known bridge marks
the start of the Lincoln Woods
trailhead

several more streams that can be strategically rock-hopped. You can take off your hiking boots and put on your water shoes to cross as well.

After hiking for a little over 8 miles from the trailhead, you will finally reach Camp 13—the Thirteen Falls backcountry campsite. There is a composting toilet here, handy if you really need to go. The first set of falls is found by bushwhacking from Franconia Brook Trail about 0.1 mile south of Camp 13. There is no trail, so you just have to start going downhill until you reach the water and gauge from there which way to go. The first and second set of waterfalls are only 20 feet apart, so you'll likely see one or the other immediately.

The lowermost falls is likely the hardest to get to since it brings you 100 feet off the trail to reach the water's edge. The pool is the biggest of the bunch and absolutely breathtaking to see. The second-lowest falls and pool are just 20 feet upstream and can be accessed by walking along the river's edge. The third waterfall has no pool at the bottom, so it can be skipped.

To access the fourth and fifth waterfalls, get back on Franconia Brook Trail and then take a left onto Lincoln Brook Trail. You'll cross a branch of Franconia Brook and then continue on the trail on the other side. About 150 feet after the crossing, turn left and bushwhack for 60 feet until you reach the brook. This is where you'll find water sliding down and plunging 10 feet into a small pool.

When you're done at the fourth falls, get back on the Lincoln Brook Trail. The fifth set of waterfalls is 100 feet upstream from the fourth falls, although it cannot be seen from there. Walk another 100 feet along the Lincoln Brook Trail and then head out into the woods on your left for only about 25 feet to where the fifth set of falls should be. This waterfall has a mixture of plunges, slides, and cascades, making for a dramatic-looking landscape. The pool at the bottom is a bit longer and narrower than the others, but just as great to take a dip in. And after more than 8 miles of walking, the cold water will feel good on your weary muscles.

Make sure you allow enough time to truly enjoy all four pools. I stayed for almost 2 hours and only swam in one of the pools. When you're finished, head back to Franconia Brook Trail and make the long trek south to Lincoln Woods Trail. Even when you get back on that flat trail, it's still nearly 3 miles back to the trailhead. When you round the corner and see the bridge over the Pemigewasset River, it'll be a welcome sight.

MILES AND DIRECTIONS

0.00 Start from the Lincoln Woods trailhead in front and to the left of the ranger station.

0.10 Cross over the bridge to get to the northwestern side of the Pemigewasset River. Turn right to head north.

1.45 Ford/rock-hop the small stream where the bridge is out and cannot be accessed.

1.90 Cross over another small stream.

2.90 Stay straight when you reach the intersection with Franconia Falls Trail. Cross the bridge over Franconia Brook.

3.40 Stream crossing.

3.60 Stream crossing.

As you get further into the Pemigewasset Wilderness, the trail becomes something from a fantastical realm.

One of a series of pools
along Thirteen Falls

4.15   Stream crossing.

4.60   Intersection with Lincoln Brook Trail.

4.70   Pass by wetlands on your right (potential to see moose in this area and lots of mosquitoes).

5.40   Stream crossing.

6.35   Stream crossing.

7.50   Stream crossing.

8.20   Arrive at Camp 13. Walk around Franconia Brook and Lincoln Brook to hit up all four swimming holes along Thirteen Falls. This adds about 0.4 mile to this trek and is included in the total mileage.

8.60   Head back down Franconia Brook Trail.

9.30   Stream crossing.

10.15   Stream crossing.

11.10   Stream crossing.

11.80   Pass by the wetlands, now on your left. Keep an extra eye out for any wildlife.

11.90   Intersection with Lincoln Brook Trail.

12.35   Stream crossing.

12.90   Stream crossing.

13.10   Stream crossing.

13.60   Cross over the bridge across Franconia Brook.

The lowermost pool at Thirteen Falls

14.60 Stream crossing.

15.05 Stream crossing.

16.40 Cross over the bridge spanning the Pemigewasset River.

16.50 Arrive back at the trailhead and ranger station.

38 **MOUNTAIN POND**

For a bit of remoteness without having to walk too far, look no further than Mountain Pond. It's perfect as a first-time backpacking trip, with kids or just yourself. The serenity and peacefulness of Mountain Pond allows for an abundant amount of wildlife, including loons and black bears.

Start: At the Mountain Pond trailhead
Elevation gain: 60 feet
Distance: 2.6-mile lollipop
Difficulty: Easy to moderate
Hiking time: About 1 hour
Fees and permits: No fee required
Trail contact: White Mountain National Forest, 71 White Mountain Dr., Campton, NH 03223; (603) 536-6100; www.fs.usda.gov/recarea/whitemountain/recarea/?recid=74891
Dog-friendly: Allowed on leash

Trail surface: Dirt and rocks/roots
Land status: US Forest Service
Nearest town: Jackson, NH
Other trail users: Hunters
Temperature of water: 65°F
Body of water: Mountain Pond
Water availability: None
Maps: White Mountain National Forest map
Toilets: No
Wheelchair compatibility: No
Family-friendly: Yes

FINDING THE TRAILHEAD

From Concord, take I-93 North for approximately 30 miles. Take exit 23 for NH-104/NH-132 toward Meredith/New Hampton. Merge onto NH-104 East/NH-132 North for approximately 8 miles. Turn left onto US-3 North, and then after 1 mile, turn right onto NH-25 East/Winnipesaukee Street. Drive for 19 miles and then turn left onto NH-113 East. Stay on NH-113 for 5 miles, then turn left onto NH-16 North for almost 12 miles. Turn left to stay on NH-16 North and drive for an additional 9.3 miles. Turn right onto Town Hall Road; after approximately 6 miles, the road forks. Take the right fork onto Slippery Brook Road. Continue for approximately 0.5 mile; the parking lot will be on the right. GPS: N44 10.2174', W71 5.3028'

THE HIKE

I did this hike with my kid and stayed overnight to experience all the aspects of Mountain Pond. The trail into the camping area, on the northern side of the pond, is only about a mile. It was an ideal distance for my kiddo at the time, and close enough to the trailhead that if something went wrong, we could get back easily.

Start the trail at the Mountain Pond trailhead off Slippery Brook Road (a dirt road). You'll see dispersed camping along Slippery Brook Road as you drive to the trailhead. It's a popular area for this recreational activity. The trail forks around the 0.3-mile mark. It doesn't matter which way you go around the pond, as there are swimming spots on both sides of it.

I'd suggest taking a left if you are backpacking in the area so you can snag the campsite where the first swimming hole is. This is where my kiddo and I stayed overnight and it was gorgeous. We fell asleep to the haunting calls of the loons while a full moon hung over the glassy pond. We awoke to an orange glow coming through our tent and

MOUNTAIN POND

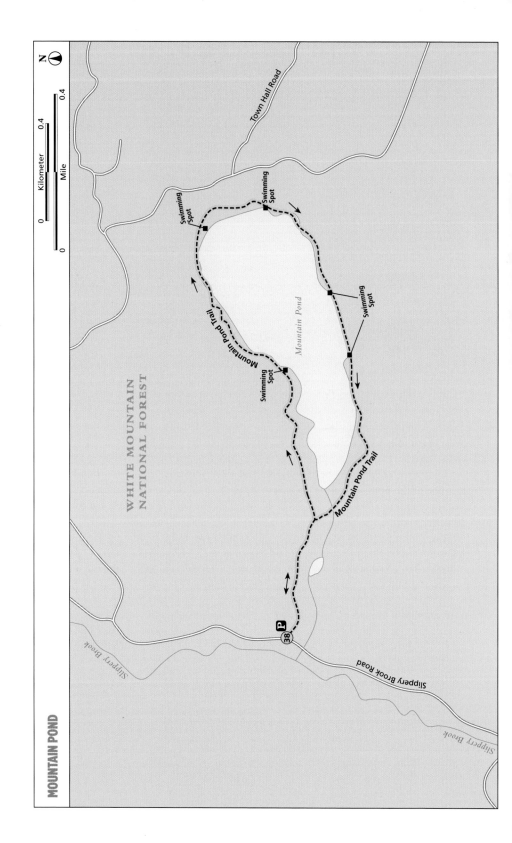

WHITE MOUNTAIN
NATIONAL FOREST

Town Hall Road

Swimming Spot

Swimming Spot

Swimming Spot

Swimming Spot

Mountain Pond

Mountain Pond Trail

Mountain Pond Trail

Slippery Brook

Slippery Brook Road

Slippery Brook

P
38

N

Kilometer
0   0.4

Mile
0   0.4

Sunrise over the pond

songbirds filling our ears. The swimming here is remote, however, and there is no beach area where it's easy to get in and out.

Watch out for leeches because, yes, they are found in this pond. If you're squeamish about them, then Mountain Pond will likely not be a favorite of yours. There are also tons of water snakes (completely harmless) in the water, which might frighten some folks.

Continue on the trail by heading right from the first swimming hole to round the eastern side of the pond. There are two swimming spots on this side where you can wade in and dip your toes a bit more. One is at the northern end of the east bank, while the other is at the southern end—at the 1.15-mile and 1.4-mile marks, respectively. Continue walking along the southern side of the lake, where two more swimming spots are found just off the trail—one at 1.65 miles and the other at 1.8 miles from the start of the hike.

When you've enjoyed all the swimming spots, head west on the trail until you close the loop at the trail fork. Take a left to head back to the parking area and trailhead.

LOONS ARE EXCELLENT DIVERS

Loons are frequent inhabitants of Mountain Pond, and you'll likely hear their haunting calls if you decide to stay overnight. If you watch them closely, you'll notice they disappear under the water only to pop back up a few hundred feet away. They swim underwater to catch (and eat!) fish with their sharp beaks. They have backward-facing projections on the roof of their mouth/beak that help keep prey in place once caught. Part of what makes them excellent swimmers is that they have solid bones, unlike most birds, which have hollow bones. This makes them heavier and better equipped to dive after prey.

The waters of Mountain Pond might be chilly, but the views are gorgeous

MILES AND DIRECTIONS

0.00 Start at the Mountain Pond trailhead.

0.30 Veer left at the fork.

0.80 Arrive at a backcountry tent site and the first swimming spot.

1.15 Reach the second swimming spot.

1.40 Reach the third swimming spot.

1.65 Reach the fourth swimming spot.

1.80 Reach the fifth and final swimming spot.

2.30 Veer left at the fork.

2.60 Arrive back at the trailhead.

39 EMERALD POOL

Emerald Pool got its name for a very specific reason—all you have to do is take one look at the body of water and you'll know. The crystal-clear waters of Charles Brook take on a distinct greenish hue as the river cascades into Emerald Pool. Visitors can thank the granite slabs that line the magical waters for their magnificent color and not some malicious algae taking over the brook. Tread lightly in this area to ensure the beauty of the landscape is maintained.

Start: At the Baldface trailhead
Elevation gain: 215 feet
Distance: 1.6 miles out and back
Difficulty: Easy
Hiking time: About 1 hour
Fees and permits: No fee required
Trail contact: White Mountain National Forest, 71 White Mountain Dr., Campton, NH 03223; (603) 536-6100; www.fs.usda .gov/recarea/whitemountain/ recarea/?recid=74509
Dog-friendly: Allowed on leash

Trail surface: Dirt
Land status: US Forest Service
Nearest town: North Chatham, NH
Other trail users: None
Temperature of water: 65°F
Body of water: Charles Brook
Water availability: None
Maps: White Mountain National Forest topographical map
Toilets: Yes, at the trailhead
Wheelchair compatibility: No
Family-friendly: Yes

FINDING THE TRAILHEAD

From Portsmouth, follow NH-16 North/US-4 West for approximately 5 miles to where it turns into NH-16 North. Follow NH-16 North for approximately 71 miles. Continue straight onto NH-113 East/East Main Street for 2 miles. Turn left onto US-302 West. After 1 mile, turn right onto East Conway Road. Follow this road for approximately 6.5 miles; it then turns into West Fryeburg Road. After 9.5 miles, take a slight right onto Stow Road for approximately 3 miles. At this point, the road turns into Main Road. Follow Main Road for approximately 2.5 miles. Parking is on your right, where about 15 cars are able to park. If the lot is full, you can park on the side of the road, but ensure that your vehicle is completely off the paved part of the road. GPS: N44 14.2902', W71 0.9684'

THE HIKE

On any given summer weekend, the parking at the Baldface trailhead can be overrun with vehicles. This is a popular trail and the starting point for two 3,000-footers (summits that are at least 3,000 feet above sea level). However, if you are able to head there during the week, early in the day, or later in the evening, you will likely be greeted with very few fellow hikers.

Start your hike across the road from the trailhead parking, where you will see a trail sign indicating the Baldface Circle Trail. Stay straight when you reach a fork about 250 feet from the trailhead—do not go left. The trail is fairly wide, with many evergreens lining both sides. This also means the ground is covered in pine needles and can be slippery in all types of weather. As with most trails in New Hampshire, there are also multiple roots protruding from the surface that are easily tripped over.

EMERALD POOL

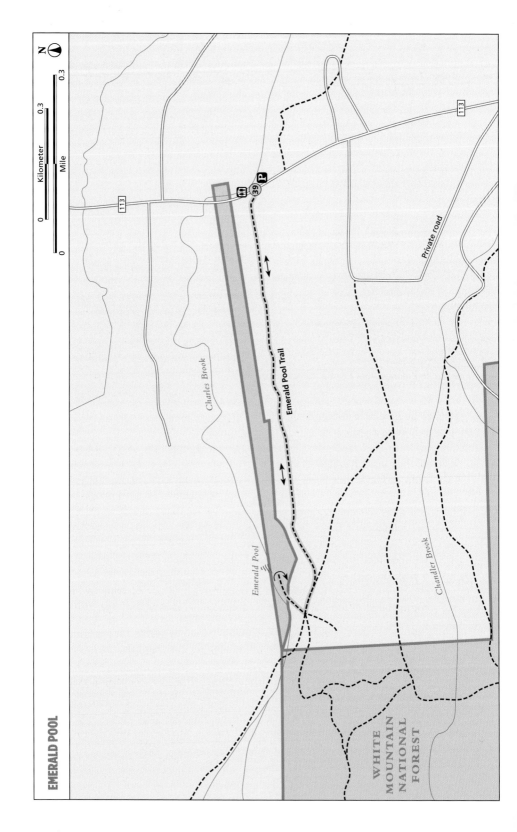

N

Kilometer
0   0.3

Mile
0   0.3

Charles Brook

Emerald Pool

Emerald Pool Trail

113

39

P

Private road

Chandler Brook

WHITE
MOUNTAIN
NATIONAL
FOREST

113

The hike to Emerald Pool takes a sharp right turn from the trail

At around the 0.4-mile mark, you will reach a stand of beautiful birch trees. If you happen to be here later in the fall for a colder dip in the water, the leaves will be a magnificent yellow that illuminates the sun already streaming down. Raised boardwalks are also scattered throughout the trail in areas most prone to mud and oversaturated soil.

You will then reach a junction at 0.7 mile; turn right to follow the sign toward Emerald Pool. You can make this a tougher hike by heading up to North Baldface or South Baldface from this spot. But if you are just coming here for the swimming hole, head right. It is a short descent to Charles Brook and the waiting Emerald Pool. There are many social trails around this area, but try to avoid them at all costs. Simply make your way down to the pool using the most obvious trail.

If it has rained recently, the rocks surrounding the pool can be very slippery and dangerous to walk on because of the amount of algae that clings to the rocks. There are several rocks that look great to jump from, but although it may be tempting, jumping is not recommended, as the water is not deep enough. However, the large, flat boulders

WHAT ARE SOCIAL TRAILS?
Social trails are in abundance on this hike. Social trails are considered informal paths (i.e., ones not maintained or made by a land management agency/ owner) that have been created due to many visitors making their own way through a forest. This happens often in places where many people gather, like a swimming hole. Social trails, however, increase erosion to an area and can be detrimental to not just the trail but also the surrounding waterbodies. It's why it is so important to stay on the trail at all times. In addition, when you are around Emerald Pool, try to walk on hard surfaces like boulders and rocks.

Emerald Pool, like so many swimming holes in New England, has a greenish hue due to the granite

that surround the pool are perfect for anyone who wants to sunbathe (whenever the sun might reach through all the leaves) or relax while others swim. Once you've gotten your fill of the water, head back the way you came to return to your car.

MILES AND DIRECTIONS

0.00 Begin at the trailhead on the opposite side of the road from where you parked. Follow the yellow blazes.

0.05 At the fork, stay straight. Do *not* go left.

0.40 Meander through a stand of birch trees.

0.70 Follow the sign and turn right to head to Emerald Pool.

0.80 Reach Emerald Pool. Turn around and go back the way you came.

0.90 Reach the junction with the Baldface Trail. Turn left to head back toward the trailhead.

1.20 Revel in the surrounding birch trees.

1.55 Stay straight at the fork.

1.60 Arrive back at the parking lot by crossing the road once again.

40 RATTLE RIVER FALLS

This swimming hole is the hidden gem of White Mountain National Forest. It follows part of the Appalachian Trail and brings you through some of the most beautiful sections of river in the region. With its ease of access and epic beauty, it's surprising that this swimming hole isn't more popular or well-known.

Start: At the Rattle River trailhead
Elevation gain: 520 feet
Distance: 3.4 miles out and back
Difficulty: Moderate
Hiking time: About 2 hours
Fees and permits: No fee required
Trail contact: White Mountain National Forest, 71 White Mountain Dr., Campton, NH 03223; (603) 536-6100; www.fs.usda .gov/recarea/whitemountain/ recarea/?recid=74509
Dog-friendly: Allowed on leash

Trail surface: Dirt and rocks/roots
Land status: US Forest Service
Nearest town: Gorham, NH
Other trail users: None
Temperature of water: 65°F
Body of water: Rattle River
Water availability: None
Maps: White Mountain National Forest topographical map
Toilets: No
Wheelchair compatibility: No
Family-friendly: Yes

FINDING THE TRAILHEAD

From Concord, take I-93 North for approximately 74 miles. Take exit 35 for US-3 North toward Lancaster/Twin Mountain. Continue on US-3 North for 12 miles and then turn right onto NH-115 North. Drive for an additional 10 miles and turn right onto US-2 East. Travel for around 17.5 miles until you reach the parking lot on your right. There is enough parking for around 20 cars. GPS: N44 10.2174', W71 5.3028'

THE HIKE

I'll be honest; I debated whether or not to include this swimming hole in the guide. Of all the swimming holes in this book, Rattle River Falls is, without a doubt, my all-time favorite. There's nothing super extraordinary about it other than being secluded, relatively unknown, and ideal for most skill levels.

You start the trail at the Appalachian trailhead off US-2 to head south toward the Rattle River Shelter. About 0.4 mile in, you'll reach a fork. Make sure to stay right to continue on the Appalachian Trail, which follows the Rattle River almost the entire time.

When you get just over 1.5 miles in, you'll reach the Rattle River Shelter, where you can camp overnight. There is also a large backcountry camping area to the left up the hill. From the shelter, turn right to head down toward the river on a spur trail. There is a small swimming hole here, but opt for the one that is slightly downstream.

Get into the river at this point to make your way down to the falls and second swimming hole. The woods around the river are currently undergoing some revegetation efforts. There are signs on many trees asking hikers to steer clear of the area while this is going on. Please adhere to these warnings so people can keep coming to this place for generations to come.

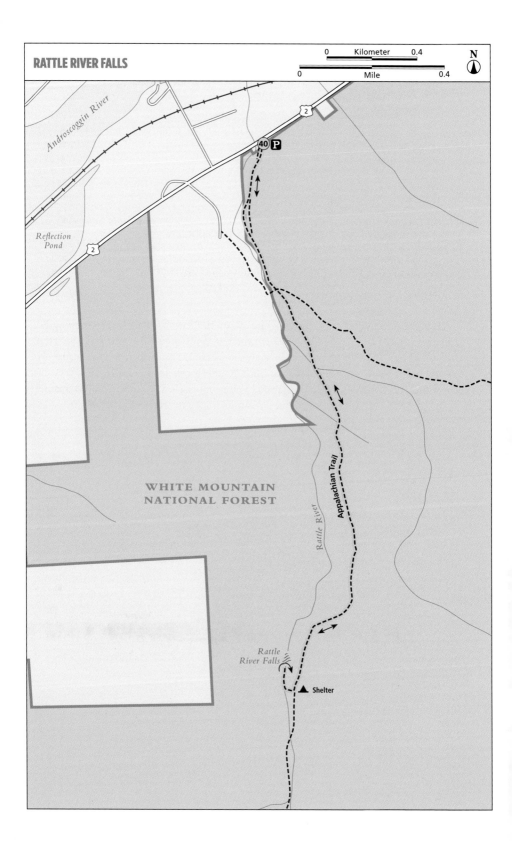

RATTLE RIVER FALLS

Kilometer
0   0.4
Mile
0   0.4

N

Androscoggin River

Reflection
Pond

2

40 P

WHITE MOUNTAIN
NATIONAL FOREST

Rattle River

Appalachian Trail

Rattle
River Falls

▲ Shelter

The second swimming hole and falls are about 100 feet from the first swimming hole at the base of the spur trail. This is where the real fun begins. The vertical drop is only about 12 feet, but it slides down gradually over the course of 75 feet, which means—you guessed it—natural waterslides! That's right. Rattle River Falls is home to a very cool natural waterslide that falls into a beautifully clear pool below. You and your companions (both big and little ones) will have fun for hours in this natural playground.

You can stay overnight at the Rattle River Shelter

The pools of Rattle River Falls as seen from above

The upper pool at Rattle River Falls has some natural waterslides

Head back up the river and the bank on your left to get back to the shelter. Dry off and change if you desire before heading north along the Appalachian Trail to get back to your car.

MILES AND DIRECTIONS

0.00 Start at the Appalachian trailhead off US-2 and head south.

0.40 Veer right at the fork.

1.60 Arrive at the Rattle River Shelter. Take a right to head down to the water.

1.70 Reach Rattle River Falls. Enjoy and then head back up the bank to the shelter.

1.80 Take a left to head north on the Appalachian Trail.

3.00 Stay straight/slightly left to stay on the Appalachian Trail.

3.40 Arrive back at the trailhead.

Looking upriver at
the lower pool of
Rattle River Falls

MAINE

Step Falls provides multiple
swimming holes along its length

41 RATTLESNAKE POOL

Being afraid of snakes shouldn't deter you from this backcountry swimming hole, since technically there are no rattlesnakes in the area. Instead, you'll find a beautiful waterfall plunging into an emerald-green pool thanks to the granite rocks surrounding it. A sort of cousin to Emerald Pool, Rattlesnake Pool holds its own by delivering extraordinary beauty in a deep pool perfect for swimming.

Start: At the end of Shell Pond Road
Elevation gain: 235 feet
Distance: 2.1 miles out and back
Difficulty: Easy to moderate
Hiking time: About 1 hour
Fees and permits: No fee required
Trail contact: White Mountain National Forest, 71 White Mountain Dr., Campton, NH; (603) 536-6100; www.fs.usda.gov/recarea/whitemountain/recarea/?recid=74581
Dog-friendly: Allowed on leash

Trail surface: Dirt and rocks/roots
Land status: US Forest Service
Nearest town: Stow, ME
Other trail users: None
Temperature of water: 65°F
Body of water: Rattlesnake Brook
Water availability: None
Maps: White Mountain National Forest topographical map
Toilets: No
Wheelchair compatibility: No
Family-friendly: Yes

FINDING THE TRAILHEAD

From Portland, take I-295 South/US-1 South toward South Portland. Take exit 1 toward I-95 North. Merge onto Maine Turnpike and take the immediate exit toward Jetport. Use the left 2 lanes to turn left onto Maine Mall Road. After 0.5 mile, turn right onto Cummings Road; in another 0.5 mile, turn left onto Running Hill Road. Travel approximately 2 miles and turn right onto ME-114 North. In 3 miles, take the second exit at the traffic circle to get onto ME-112 South. Drive another 3.5 miles to the next traffic circle. Take the second exit to merge onto ME-25 West/Ossipee Trail East. Drive on ME-25 West for approximately 8 miles and then turn right onto ME-113 North for 30 miles. Turn right onto Main Street and continue for 4.5 miles. Turn left onto Fish Street for 3 miles, then turn right onto North Fryeburg Road. After 1.6 miles the road turns into Stow Road. In another 5 miles, the road turns into Main Road. Drive 4 miles on Main Road and then turn right onto Stone House Road, which immediately turns into Shell Pond Road. Drive for about 1 mile, until the road ends at a small parking area and gate. Park in the small parking lot (enough for 5 cars) and walk the road to get to the trailhead. GPS: N44 15.1176', W70 59.4414'

THE HIKE

Historically, the mountains of western Maine were home to timber rattlesnakes, although the population had always been very low. The more likely reason this place is called Rattlesnake Brook/Pool is due to the curvy nature of the river itself.

You start the trail at the end of Shell Pond Road, where the closed gate indicates you need to park. The first part of the trail is on private property, but the landowners have always allowed access to the public. To ensure these lands will stay accessible, please stay on the trail and do not go to the house that's at the end of the dirt road. After 0.5 mile of walking along the dirt road, turn left onto the trail toward Rattlesnake Pool. There are signs showing you the way.

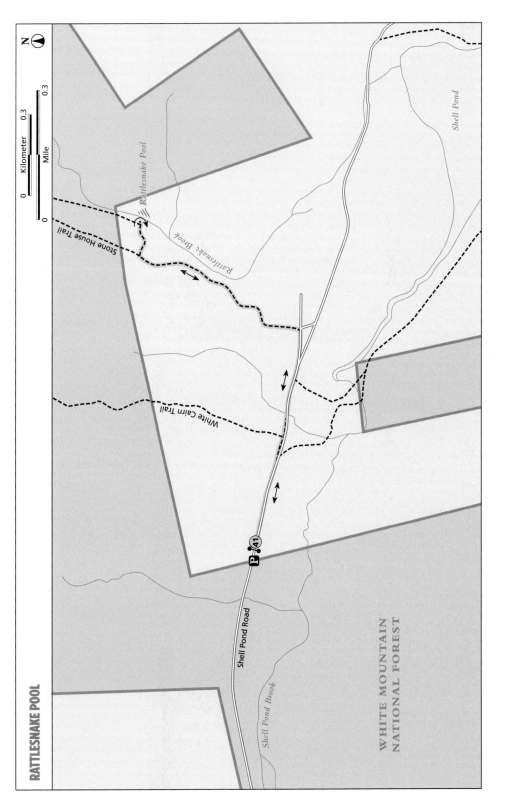

RATTLESNAKE POOL

N

0   Kilometer   0.3
0   Mile   0.3

Stone House Trail

Rattlesnake Pool

Rattlesnake Brook

White Cairn Trail

Shell Pond

P 41

Shell Pond Road

Shell Pond Brook

WHITE MOUNTAIN
NATIONAL FOREST

The emerald-green water
will mesmerize you

The trail to Rattlesnake Pool is wide and relatively root-free

You'll make your way up the trail, which steadily ascends the hill. Around the 0.7-mile mark, you'll reach a junction. Turn right to walk on the bridge that crosses Rattlesnake Brook. Here you can view the dramatic gorge that cuts through the land with the brook narrowly winding its way through the bottom. Head back the way you came and turn right to continue on the trail.

A little under a mile from the start, you'll encounter the intersection to head right, down to Rattlesnake Pool. Take this trail, and another 0.1 mile will get you down to this incredible place. Technically, the pool and surrounding land is private property, but the owners have kept this place available to the public for generations. Please do your part in ensuring it stays that way by leaving the area better than you found it.

Swim until you can't swim anymore and then head back up to the junction with the main trail. Turn left and back down toward Shell Pond Road. Turn right when you

THERE ARE NO VENOMOUS SNAKES IN MAINE

It would be quite a day if you walked along a trail in Maine and witnessed what you thought to be a venomous snake. Vacationland houses nine different species of snakes, but none of them are venomous. Maine used to be home to the timber rattlesnake (which is found in neighboring New Hampshire but in very small quantities). Timber rattlesnakes are extremely rare (so much so that they are protected by law in New Hampshire), and are also docile and highly unlikely to bite you. So even if they found their way back into Maine, it'd be unlikely to find one to bite you.

Garter snakes, however, are very common in Maine. I'm not sure why Rattlesnake Pool wasn't called "Garter Snake Pool," but perhaps the name didn't roll off the tongue as nicely. Garter snakes are completely harmless and eat nuisance creatures like insects and mice. Most of the time, you will not notice a snake on the trail. They are usually found in the grasses that border a trail, and they are more afraid of you than you are of them. Every so often, you will find a snake sunning itself on the trail. Give it a wide berth and continue on your way.

Rattlesnake Pool is deep and perfect for swimming

arrive at the dirt road and continue until you reach the small parking area on the opposite side of the gate.

MILES AND DIRECTIONS

0.00 Start from the parking area at the end of Shell Pond Road.

0.50 Turn left onto the trail into the woods. Do not go to the house on the property.

0.70 Turn right to check out the gorge that Rattlesnake Brook meanders through. Get back on the main trail to head up to the pool.

0.95 Turn right to head toward Rattlesnake Pool.

1.05 Arrive at Rattlesnake Pool. After your swim, turn around and go back the way you came.

1.15 Turn left down the main trail to head back to the trailhead.

1.60 Turn right when you reach the gravel road.

2.10 Arrive back at the trailhead.

42 SUNDAY RIVER ROAD POOLS

Why only settle for one swimming hole when you can hit up three? If you're in western Maine, take a drive along Sunday River Road and visit three distinct and unique swimming holes that will be favorites for years to come. All are located just off the road, making them a great way to spend a relaxing weekend by the water.

Start: Various points along Sunday River Road
Elevation gain: None
Distance: None
Difficulty: Easy
Hiking time: None
Fees and permits: No fee required
Trail contact: Mahoosuc Unit Reserve, Bull Branch Rd., Newry, ME 04261; (207) 778-8231; www .maine.gov/dacf/mnap/reservesys/ mahoosucs.htm
Dog-friendly: Allowed on leash

Trail surface: Gravel, dirt, and rocks/ roots
Land status: Maine Bureau of Parks and Lands
Nearest town: Sunday River, ME
Other trail users: None
Temperature of water: 65°F
Body of water: Sunday River
Water availability: None
Maps: Sunday River Road map
Toilets: No
Wheelchair compatibility: No
Family-friendly: Yes

FINDING THE TRAILHEAD

From Portland, take I-95 North for approximately 10 miles. Take exit 63 for US-202 toward Gray/Windham. Use the middle lane to turn left onto ME-115 and then immediately turn right onto ME-26A North. Travel for approximately 24.5 miles and turn left onto East Main Street, which turns into ME-26 North. Drive for 23 miles and then turn right onto Parkway Road. Shortly after, turn right onto US-2 East for 2.5 miles. Turn left onto Sunday River Road. The bridge is 3.3 miles from this point. Parking is available on both sides of the bridge. Sunday River Bridge GPS: N44 29.5374', W70 50.6022'

From Sunday River Bridge, continue on Sunday River Road for another 2.5 miles. Parking for the Sunday River Swim Area is on the right and only has 13 spaces for cars. You cannot park anywhere else and will be towed if you try. Sunday River Swim Area GPS: N44 29.8824', W70 53.3118'

From Sunday River Swim Area, continue on Sunday River Road for another 1.4 miles. Turn left onto Twin Bridges Road and immediately turn right after the bridge onto Bull Branch Road. Sometimes this road is closed for repairs, so you'll have to park on the side of the road and walk the road to the hole. If the road is clear, there is a parking area 0.75 mile down Bull Branch Road across from Frenchman's Hole. Frenchman's Hole GPS: N44 30.6354', W70 55.0974'

THE HIKE

This is more of a drive than a hike, but who's checking? Not me. Most people might know this area for its famed ski resort, but there's more to the area than shredding some powder. In the summer months, this road is rampant with swimming holes that visitors love to take advantage of.

The first swimming hole to stop at is the Sunday River Bridge. This is one of three covered bridges in this guide and, for some reason, I just can't get enough of them. There is something so "New England" about a covered bridge that it makes swimming near

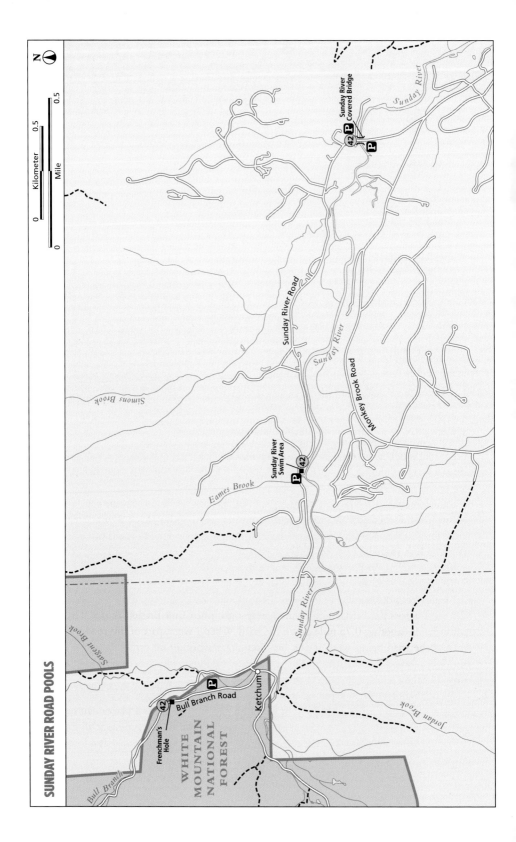

SUNDAY RIVER ROAD POOLS

You can access the river on both sides of the bridge

them that much more enjoyable. You can park on either side of the bridge and make your way down to the river. You can cross to either side by using the covered bridge, as cars are not allowed through it.

After enjoying the covered bridge, get back in your car and continue down Sunday River Road for another 2.5 miles until you reach the Sunday River Swim Area. There are enough spaces on the right-hand (north) side of the road for thirteen cars—no more. If you aren't impeding traffic, you can wait to see if any spots open up if it's full. The swimming area is just across the street and down to the river.

The last swimming hole on this road is the best one. Frenchman's Hole lies another 2.1 miles from the Sunday River Swim Area. Continue on Sunday River Road and then head left across the bridge and immediately right onto Bull Branch Road. The swimming hole is another 0.75 mile down the road. When I went, part of this road was closed due to the road being washed out, but they were working on repairs to get it quickly fixed. Just know that this road is prone to flooding and can be inaccessible to cars every now and then.

Frenchman's Hole is a plunge waterfall that plummets 10 feet into the large pool below. This is the most popular spot to swim, but more secluded places can be found both up- and downstream of this area. When you're finished swimming at all these different spots, feel free to hit them up a second time, or just head home after a long day of swimming in the epic pools.

The pool at the base of the falls is harder to get to but quite beautiful

MILES AND DIRECTIONS

0.00 Start at Sunday River Bridge. Get back in your car and drive to Sunday River Swim Area down the road.

2.50 Arrive at Sunday River Swim Area. Get in your car once again to finish the day at Frenchman's Hole, farther down Sunday River Road.

4.60 Arrive at Frenchman's Hole. Head home when you're done for the day.

43 PEBBLE BEACH

Even though this is a swimming holes book, this is the only beach in this guide where you must take a boat in order to get there. And because of that, Pebble Beach tends to be very quiet and secluded, as most folks who visit the area are headed to the golf course instead. Before you hit the beach, though, hike up Mount Kineo to take in the views of New England's second-largest lake: Moosehead Lake.

Start: At the Carriage trailhead—only accessible by boat
Elevation gain: 1,050 feet
Distance: 5.25 miles out and back
Difficulty: Strenuous
Hiking time: About 3 hours
Fees and permits: Fee required
Trail contact: Mount Kineo State Park, Maine State Parks, Bureau of Parks and Lands, 106 Hogan Rd., Ste. 7, Bangor, ME; (207) 941-4014; www .maine.gov/mountkineo
Dog-friendly: Not allowed
Trail surface: Gravel and dirt

Land status: Maine Bureau of Parks and Lands
Nearest town: Rockwood, ME
Other trail users: None
Temperature of water: 60°F
Body of water: Moosehead Lake
Water availability: At the golf course restaurant
Maps: Mount Kineo State Park trail map
Toilets: Yes, at the boat launch parking and golf course restaurant
Wheelchair compatibility: No
Family-friendly: Yes

FINDING THE TRAILHEAD
Pebble Beach is accessible by water only, with the nearest public boat launch site in Rockwood. From Bangor, take ME 15 North for approximately 36 miles until you reach Dover Foxcroft. Take a left on ME 6 (also ME 15) West for approximately 53 miles. Turn right onto Village Road toward the Town Landing. A commercial boat shuttle (fee charged) to the island leaves routinely from Rockwood in the summer months. Parking lot GPS: N45 40.6458', W69 44.3334'; beach GPS: N45 42.024', W69 43.2366'

THE HIKE
There are no accessible roads that lead to Pebble Beach. Instead, you must take a passenger ferry from the Rockwood Town Landing/boat launch to the start of the trail just across Moosehead Lake. In this region of Maine, moose outnumber people three to one, so keep an eye out on the road to the boat launch.

The ferry runs from May until October and varies in its schedule depending on the month you are hiking in. Usually, the ferry leaves every hour on the hour from around 9 a.m. to 4 p.m. Again, double-check the ferry schedule prior to your departure. The ferry only takes cash, so come prepared to pay the fee for all passengers in your party. Keep in mind when the last shuttle is scheduled to bring you back across the lake to your car. If you miss that last ferry, you will be stuck on the island and have to wait until the next morning to take the shuttle back.

Once you make it across the lake, you can do one of two things. You can take the road to the right to head to Pebble Beach, or left to hike up Mount Kineo and the 360-degree tower at the top. I suggest heading up Mount Kineo to see the gorgeous views from the

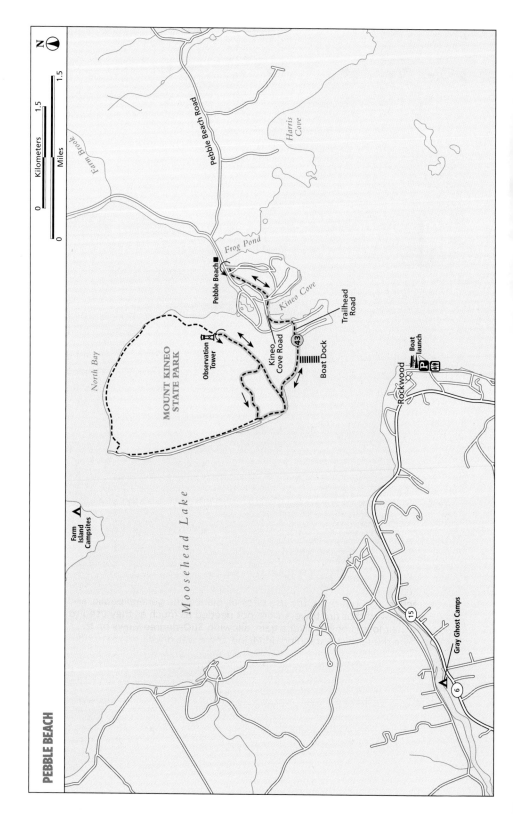

N

Kilometers
0   1.5

Miles
0   1.5

Farm Island Campsites

Moosehead Lake

North Bay

MOUNT KINEO STATE PARK

Observation Tower

Kineo Cove Road

Kineo Cove

43

Trailhead Road

Boat Dock

Pebble Beach

Frog Pond

Farm Brook

Pebble Beach Road

Harris Cove

Rockwood

Boat launch

P

15

6

Gray Ghost Camps

Views for days as you make your way to the tower atop Mount Kineo

top before ending your day at Pebble Beach. Start immediately when you get off the boat by taking a left on the Carriage Trail. After just over 0.5 mile, turn right to head up the Indian Trail. This is a slightly quicker, but much steeper way to get up the mountain.

FIRE TOWERS IN MAINE

The observation tower on top of Mount Kineo was once used in the 1960s by the Maine Forest Service. It was converted into a viewing platform after it was decommissioned. Back in the early 1900s, devastating wildfires decimated the western United States (as well as a few million acres in the Northeast). Early detection became a high priority for government officials so that the mistakes of the past were not made again.

Fire towers were extensively used over the coming decades to catch the first glimpses of any wildfires that broke out over the large swaths of forests across the United States. Each of the fire towers was manned by federal or state government staff or volunteers who were trained at spotting wildfires. There are still several active towers within the country, but many (including those in Maine) have either been decommissioned or have fallen into disrepair.

As technology improved, the use of small planes, the general public, and satellites proved that fire towers were not needed as much as they used to be. What is their loss is now a hiker's gain, allowing 360-degree views on the summits where they are still standing. In Maine, there was once upward of 155 fire towers in use within the state. Only two of those original towers are still active to this day, while fifteen more are open to the public to use.

Going up some of these fire towers isn't for the weak of heart, as many do not have closed-in rails. Those with a fear of heights might find themselves not wanting to go much farther when they reach the fire towers. Some more notable ones you can visit throughout the state include the Mount Pisgah fire tower in Winthrop, which gives visitors views of central Maine. The Mount Blue fire tower is very modern and an easier climb than many of the other fire towers available for public use.

This trail should only be attempted as an ascent. It is too steep and has too many slippery rocks, roots, and leaves for it to be considered safe as a descent. There are several spots to look out across the lake as you make your way up on the Indian Trail. You will likely need the rest, as you climb over 600 feet in under 0.5 mile—that's a consistent 12 percent grade and no easy feat. Eventually, you will see the Bridle Trail off to your left, but continue straight to head toward the observation tower. Another 0.5 mile will bring you to the base of the observation tower; 360-degree views await you at the top.

The stairs to get up the observation tower can be a little scary. The fencing and railings have large holes in them that can easily fit a small child, so please be careful with your little ones. If you don't feel safe heading up the observation tower, do not attempt it. The views that you see coming up the trail are almost as good as the ones at the top, so you would not be missing out on much.

The only way to reach Pebble Beach is by boat across Moosehead Lake

When you've soaked up enough views of the lake, climb down the observation tower and head back down Indian Trail. When you reach the junction of the Indian and Bridle Trails, turn right to get back onto Bridle Trail. Again, do not attempt to descend on Indian Trail—it is very dangerous. The trail down Bridle is much more gradual and easier on your knees, but there are no views of the lake from this side.

Eventually, you will meet back up with the Carriage Trail. Turn left and continue on the flat path that will bring you back to the boat launch. To get to Pebble Beach, head straight, with the ferry dock to your right, and then take a left onto Kineo Cove Road. At the fork, stay left onto Pebble Beach Road, which you'll follow until you reach a causeway with Frog Pond on your right and North Bay to your left. Pebble Beach is on the left-hand side.

MILES AND DIRECTIONS

0.00 Start on the level Carriage Trail by taking a left from the boat launch (away from the golf course).

0.60 Turn right onto the Indian Trail.

1.00 Stay straight to head toward the summit.

1.40 Reach the summit. Go back the way you came.

1.80 Veer right to head down the Bridle Trail.

2.35 Take a left to head back on the Carriage Trail toward the boat launch.

3.20 Pass the trailhead and keep going straight on Trailhead Road.

The trail is wide and flat as you make your way toward Pebble Beach

3.35 Take a left onto Kineo Cove Road.

3.70 Take a left at the fork to get to Pebble Beach Road.

4.20 Arrive at Pebble Beach. Once you're finished here, go back on Pebble Beach Road to head back to the dock.

4.70 Continue straight onto Kineo Cove Road.

5.05 Take a left onto Trailhead Road and continue straight.

5.20 Pass the trailhead and keep going straight.

5.25 Arrive back at the dock.

44 STEP FALLS

This small, 24-acre preserve is home to some of the most stunning cascades in western Maine. The short trail to the open ledges with water flowing down them makes this a popular area in the summertime. If you head here early though, you'll be able to snag a coveted spot for your car. Early bird gets the parking space, right?

Start: At the Step Falls trailhead
Elevation gain: 200 feet
Distance: 1.0 mile out and back
Difficulty: Easy to moderate
Hiking time: About 30 minutes
Fees and permits: No fee required; donation suggested
Trail contact: Step Falls Preserve, Mahoosuc Land Trust, PO Box 981, Bethel, ME 04217; (207) 824-3806; www.mahoosuc.org
Dog-friendly: Allowed on leash

Trail surface: Dirt and rocks/roots
Land status: Mahoosuc Land Trust
Nearest town: Bethel, ME
Other trail users: None
Temperature of water: 65°F
Body of water: Wight Brook
Water availability: None
Maps: Step Falls trail map
Toilets: Yes, at the trailhead
Wheelchair compatibility: No
Family-friendly: Yes

FINDING THE TRAILHEAD

From Portland, take I-95 North for approximately 10 miles. Take exit 63 for US-202 toward Gray/Windham. Use the middle lane to turn left onto ME-115 and then immediately turn right onto ME-26A North. Travel for approximately 24.5 miles and turn right onto Oxford Street. Travel 2.7 miles and then turn left onto East Main Street, which turns into ME-26 North. Drive for 23 miles and turn right onto Parkway Road. Shortly after, turn right onto US-2 East for 5.6 miles, then turn left onto ME-26 North for almost 8 miles. The parking lot will be on your right and can accommodate about 30 cars. You are not allowed to park on the roadway, so if the lot is full, you'll have to come back at a different time. GPS: N44 34.2834', W70 52.242'

THE HIKE

The trail to Step Falls is easy enough for most skill levels and is partly why it gets so crowded. Although there is technically no fee to enter this small preserve, the Mahoosuc Land Trust asks for a $5 donation to keep this place running smoothly. In the summer months, volunteers help in the parking lot to make sure everyone stays safe. It'd be great if more folks paid their share so this place can continue to be managed effectively.

Step Falls Trail is straightforward to follow, as there are no other trails in the area. Plus, the hordes of other visitors hiking at the preserve will likely lead you right there. About 0.25 mile in, you'll see the brook on your left. The farthest you can walk is up to the fence at the top of the falls, which is exactly 0.5 mile from the trailhead. There are many places to slide down into the pools below, and you'll likely see many visitors doing exactly that.

Do some scoping out of the falls and pools surrounding them. You'll want to choose an appropriate area depending on whom you have with you. When I went with my kiddo, there was a great pool farther down the cascades that was shallow enough for him to wade into but also deep enough to swim in if he wanted to. The farther you climb,

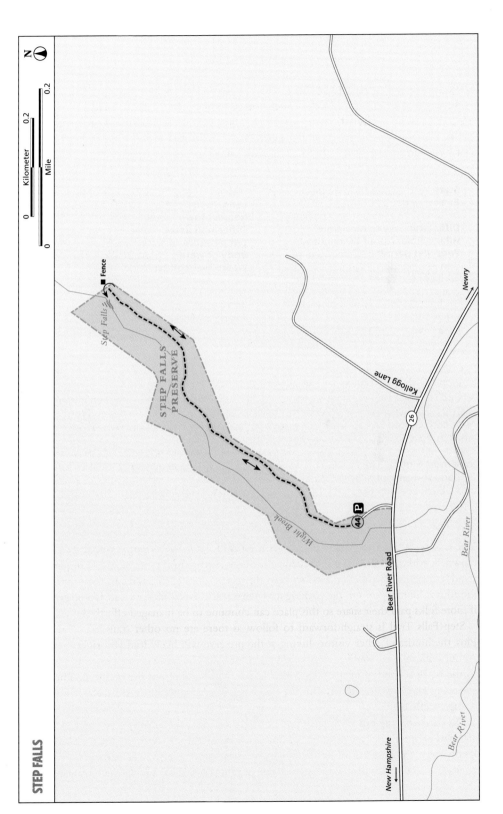

STEP FALLS

TO BUILD OR NOT BUILD ROCK CAIRNS

You'll see rock cairns all over New England's trails. Unfortunately, most of the ones you see on the trail that are seemingly put there randomly or are small in nature were done by other trail users and not the land management agencies. And although many people consider balancing rocks on top of one another a calming exercise, please refrain from building them along the trail.

For one, rock cairns are actually used on New England trails, especially above tree line where blazes aren't viable, so it can be confusing to other trail users if people start erecting rock cairns randomly. Second, when you disrupt the ground, even by simply moving a few rocks, you could potentially be disturbing insects, macroinvertebrates, reptiles, and other small organisms that might use these rocks as their home.

though, the better the views. You have gorgeous vistas of the surrounding Mahoosuc mountain range.

Make sure to keep wandering around to try out the different pools as visitors come and go. Be mindful of the people around you, especially if you are trying to slide down one of the natural waterslides. Ensure that no one is at the bottom of the pool when you attempt your slide. Enjoy every last drop of the falls and then head back on the trail to return to your car.

Looking onto the surrounding mountains at Step Falls

One of the many pools along Step Falls

MILES AND DIRECTIONS

0.00   Start at the Step Falls trailhead.

0.25   Reach the brook on your left; continue upstream.

0.50   Reach the top of the falls and the best views of the Mahoosuc mountain range. Return the way you came.

1.00   Arrive back at the small parking lot.

45 BABB'S COVERED BRIDGE

The last covered bridge in this guide is a gorgeous one that has had some unfortunate events happen to it over the years. Despite its rocky history, the covered bridge is still going strong as a swimming hole and is a great option for anyone who wants to escape the city and get away from Maine beaches.

Start: At Babb's Covered Bridge
Elevation gain: None
Distance: None
Difficulty: Easy
Hiking time: About 5 minutes
Fees and permits: No fee required
Trail contact: Maine Department of Transportation, 16 Statehouse Station, Augusta, ME 04333; (207) 624-3000; www.maine.gov/mdot/historicbridges/coveredbridges/babbsbridge
Dog-friendly: Allowed on leash

Trail surface: Sand and dirt
Land status: Maine Department of Transportation
Nearest town: Gorham and Windham, ME
Other trail users: None
Temperature of water: 70°F
Body of water: Presumpscot River
Water availability: None
Maps: Gorham/Windham road map
Toilets: No
Wheelchair compatibility: No
Family-friendly: Yes

FINDING THE TRAILHEAD
From Portland, head northwest on VT-25 for just over 11 miles. Turn left onto Covered Bridge Road/Hurricane Road and continue for 0.4 mile. You can park before you enter the covered bridge on the left-hand side. Or go over the covered bridge and park on the left-hand side after. GPS: N43 45.9636', W70 26.8776'

THE HIKE
There are a few spots available to park and scramble down to the water beneath Babb's Covered Bridge for a dip in the Presumpscot River. Wherever you park, head down on either the eastern or western banks. Do not attempt to climb down to the southwestern side, as this is private property. There are signs warning to stay away from the area.

The northwestern side is much steeper than either of the eastern banks but has the most rope swings. If that's what you're after, then head down to the western side. If not, the eastern banks offer a much more gradual way down to the water. There's also a small beach where you can sit with your kiddos.

The bridge separates the towns of Gorham and Windham—both of which are very proud of this bridge. Unfortunately, it's had some tumultuous history over the years. The original bridge (which was the oldest at the time) was burned down by vandals in 1973, and ever since, the bridge seems to be plagued with more and more vandalism every year. It's been graffitied, had holes poked in the roof, and was even damaged by a snowplow.

Fortunately, it remains open as a swimming hole to this day despite others' attempts at shutting it down. Be respectful while you're here, especially near any private property. Don't walk on private property, even if there's a rope swing you really want to try out. There are plenty of others to choose from. Lastly, use caution here, as the current can pick

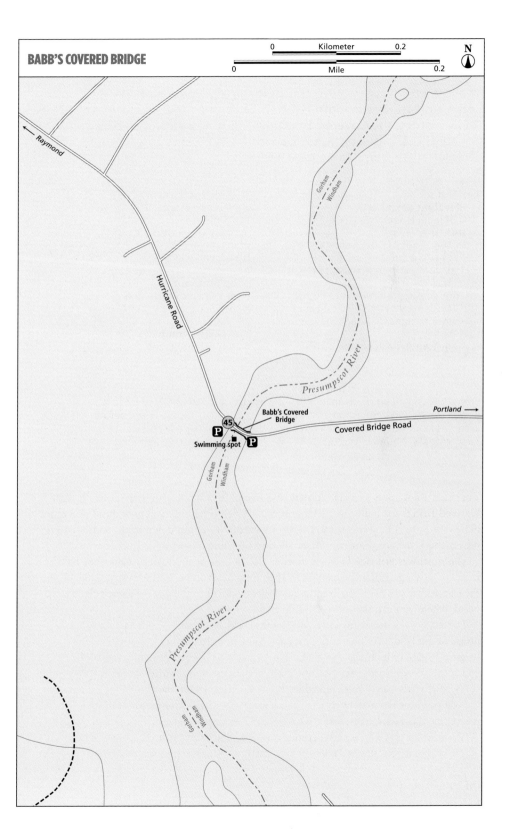

BABB'S COVERED BRIDGE

0   Kilometer   0.2
0   Mile   0.2

N

Raymond

Hurricane Road

Gorham
Windham

Presumpscot River

Portland →

Babb's Covered
Bridge

45

Covered Bridge Road

Swimming spot

Gorham
Windham

Presumpscot River

Gorham
Windham

The eastern side has more gradual
steps and areas to sunbathe

The view of Babb's Covered Bridge from the road

up quickly and without warning. The river narrows right where the bridge crosses it, so water tends to move faster here than in other sections along the river.

MILES AND DIRECTIONS

0.00 Park at any of the parking areas around the bridge and make your way down to the river.

46 **COOS CANYON**

This spot is a great option for people of all ages and skill levels. Many thrill-seekers risk climbing down the canyon or along the cliffs to jump into the deep water below. Others go upstream of the falls to wade and play in the shallower waters. No matter your adventure level, Coos Canyon does not disappoint.

Start: At the parking lot at Coos Canyon
Elevation gain: None
Distance: None
Difficulty: Easy
Hiking time: About 5 minutes
Fees and permits: No fee required
Trail contact: Coos Canyon Rest Area, Natural Resources Council of Maine, 3 Wade St., Augusta, ME 04330; (207) 622-3101; www.nrcm .org/explore-maine-map/coos -canyon-swift-river

Dog-friendly: Allowed on leash
Trail surface: Grass and rock slabs
Land status: Natural Resources Council of Maine
Nearest town: Byron, ME
Other trail users: None
Temperature of water: 65°F
Body of water: Swift River
Water availability: None
Maps: Byron road map
Toilets: Yes, across the bridge
Wheelchair compatibility: No
Family-friendly: Yes

FINDING THE TRAILHEAD

From Augusta, head west on US-202 West for approximately 11 miles. Turn right onto Western Avenue, which turns into ME-133 North after 0.4 mile. After 1 mile, take a slight left to stay on ME-133 North for an additional 6 miles. Turn left onto ME-219 West for 5.7 miles and then right onto ME-108 West. Travel for almost 22 miles and then turn right onto North Main Street. Make an immediate left onto US-2 West and travel for 4.6 miles. Turn right onto ME-17 West/Roxbury Road for 13.2 miles. The parking lot for Coos Canyon will be on the right. GPS: N44 43.2492', W70 37.9062'

A child dips their feet into the frigid water

COOS CANYON

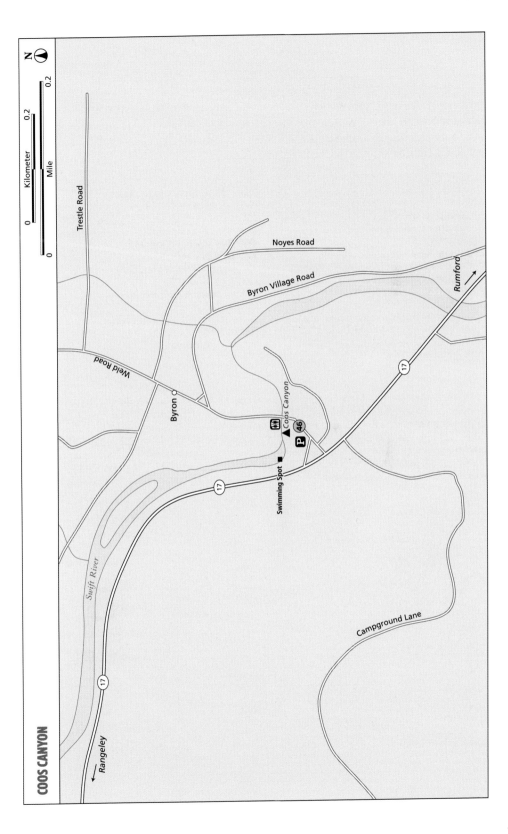

N

Kilometer
0   0.2

Mile
0   0.2

Trestle Road

Noyes Road

Byron Village Road

Rumford

Weld Road

Byron

Coos Canyon

17

Swift River

17

Rangeley

Swimming Spot

P

45

17

Campground Lane

Looking down at Coos Canyon from the bridge crossing the river

THE HIKE

The swimming hole along Coos Canyon occurs at the Coos Canyon Rest Area. You can park your car in the parking lot and then make your way down the big slabs to the edge of the river. The parking lot spits you out on top of the falls, so if you want to get to the deep swimming hole, head to the right, down the rock slabs.

This part is not for the faint of heart. The cliffs tower above the deep river below and the rocks can be slippery. But on hot, dry days, the cliffs are just too tempting not to jump from. You'll see a lot of teenagers jumping from either side of the canyon walls often. The pool is deep between the canyon walls, so there is little risk of hitting your head or anything else on the bottom of the river.

Those with younger children or not as much adventure in their blood can head upstream to some shallower sections along the Swift River. There are still some deeper pools that you can swim in but nothing as drastic as the one below the falls.

MILES AND DIRECTIONS

0.00 Park at the large parking area and make your way down to the river.

47 SMALLS FALLS

There's nothing small about Small Falls in northwestern Maine. This random rest area is an ideal spot to rest on your trek to the northern wilderness of Maine or to check off this swimming hole from your list. The falls come barreling over the cliff into a magical pool below, perfect for soaking up the sun's rays and the crisp water of the Sandy River.

Start: At the Smalls Falls trailhead
Elevation gain: 50 feet
Distance: 0.5 mile out and back
Difficulty: Easy
Hiking time: About 15 minutes
Fees and permits: No fee required
Trail contact: Smalls Falls Rest Area, Rangeley Lakes Heritage Trust, 2424 Main St., Rangeley, ME 04970; (207) 864-7321; https://rlht.org/smalls-falls
Dog-friendly: Allowed on leash
Trail surface: Dirt, rocks/roots, and wooden bridge

Land status: Rangeley Lakes Heritage Trust
Nearest town: Rangeley, NH
Other trail users: None
Temperature of water: 65°F
Body of water: Sandy River
Water availability: None
Maps: Rangeley road map
Toilets: Yes, in the picnic area
Wheelchair compatibility: No
Family-friendly: Yes

FINDING THE TRAILHEAD

From Augusta, head north on ME-27 North for 23.5 miles. Turn left onto US-2 West and drive for approximately 10 miles. Turn right onto Bridge Street and then take another right onto Town Farm Road. Travel for just over 3 miles and turn left onto ME-4 North. Drive for almost 25 miles until you see the sign for the Smalls Falls Rest Area and Trailhead. The parking lot can fit around 20 cars; an overflow lot is just off ME-4. GPS: N44 51.4818', W70 30.7866'

THE HIKE

You might get lucky and be able to park at the main trailhead right next to the stairs that bring you down to Smalls Falls. If you get here later in the day though, you might be stuck in the overflow lot that's just off ME-4. Luckily, even if you end up here, it's not a far walk to the main trailhead.

Restrooms are found along the dirt road as you make your way to the main trailhead. In addition to the primary parking area, there are also several spots next to picnic areas for day-use visitors to use. When you make it to the main parking lot, head left down the stone steps to cross the bridge over the water. I suggest hiking up to the top of the falls before you think about swimming. For one, it's a beautiful overlook, and second, it's good to scope out the area before you wade in.

Head back the way you came, and just before you reach the bridge, take a left to drop down to the water. Change into your swimsuit and wade into the water here. You can walk a little way out before the water starts to get a bit deeper. Once you're in, feel free to swim over to the deep pool beneath the waterfall. Most folks who visit this area don't swim to the base of the falls. They stick to the bridge and take photos from there. So if

SMALLS FALLS

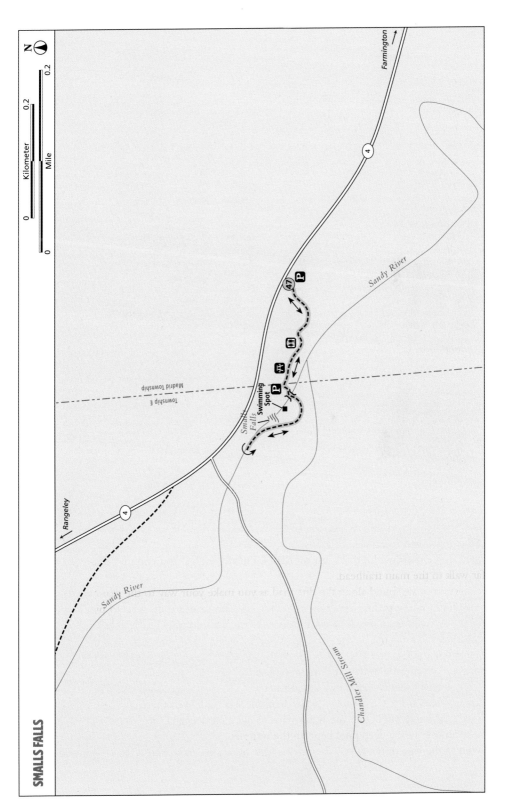

N

Kilometer
0   0.2   0.2

Mile
0   0.2

Rangeley

4

Sandy River

Smalls Falls

Swimming Spot

P

Township E
Madrid Township

P

47

P

Sandy River

Chandler Mill Stream

4

Farmington

The pool at the base of the waterfall is ideal for swimming

The bridge from the parking lot across Sandy River

you are one of the few who do make it into the pool, you'll experience a view that not many tend to see.

When you're done, make your way back to the bridge and hop out of the water. Dry off here or walk back to your car and change into some dry clothes. If you've brought food and one of the picnic areas is free, set up a gourmet dinner before you go for round two at the swimming hole!

MILES AND DIRECTIONS

0.00 If you find yourself at the overflow lot just off ME-4, start there and head down the gravel road to the trailhead.

0.10 Reach the main parking lot and trailhead.

HOW MOOSE ACT IF THEY'RE MAD

Despite how calm they might look, moose are not as friendly as you might think. In fact, I would rather encounter a black bear on the trail than a moose. In the years I have been an ecologist and an outdoor enthusiast, I have always equated moose with erratic behavior. But there are a few ways to know if you are making a moose mad or if they might charge you. Here are the signs:

- Laying their ears back.
- Hair on the back of their neck or hips is standing up.
- Smacking their lips.
- Showing the whites of their eyes.
- Tossing their heads erratically.
- Urinating on their back legs (eww).
- Or simply just charging at you. If that's the case, I hope you brought a change of swim trunks.

A child tests the water

0.15   Cross over the bridge to get to the southern side of the river.

0.25   Reach the top of the falls. Head back down to access the swimming hole.

0.30   Turn left to hike down to the water. Wade in, then swim over to the deep hole below the waterfall.

0.35   Cross back over the wooden bridge when you're done swimming.

0.40   Reach the main trailhead and parking lot. If you parked in the overflow lot, continue on the dirt road to return to your car.

0.50   Arrive back at the overflow parking lot.

48 BOOTH'S QUARRY

Travel by car and then by boat to reach this secluded swimming hole that is rarely overrun with visitors. Booth's Quarry provides swimming enthusiasts with large rock slabs to sunbathe on and deep water to tread water in for days. The views of the Atlantic Ocean on clear days are also a reason to visit this beautiful swimming hole.

Start: At the small parking lot at Booth's Quarry
Elevation gain: None
Distance: None
Difficulty: Easy
Hiking time: About 5 minutes
Fees and permits: No fee required
Trail contact: Vinalhaven Land Trust, 12 Skoog Park Rd., Vinalhaven, ME 04863; (207) 863-2543; https://vinalhavenlandtrust.org/town-parks
Dog-friendly: Not allowed

Trail surface: Sand and rock slabs
Land status: Vinalhaven Land Trust
Nearest town: Vinalhaven, ME
Other trail users: None
Temperature of water: 70°F
Body of water: Booth's Quarry Pond
Water availability: None
Maps: Vinalhaven road map
Toilets: No
Wheelchair compatibility: No
Family-friendly: Yes

FINDING THE TRAILHEAD

From Augusta, go east on ME-17 East for approximately 40 miles and then turn right onto North Main Street. Turn right onto Rankin Street after 1 mile and then left onto Union after a few hundred feet. Drive another 0.2 mile and turn left onto Lindsey Street and then make an immediate left onto Main Street. Another few hundred feet and you'll turn right at Talbot Avenue and continue on Port Terminal Road to wait for the ferry at Rockland Ferry Services.

Ferries from Rockland to Vinalhaven usually leave every 1 hour and 45 minutes from 7 a.m. until the last ferry at 4:30 p.m. This changes seasonally though. Take the 1 hour and 15 minute ride to Vinalhaven. From the ferry terminal drive northeast on West Main Street toward Sands Road for almost 1 mile. West Main Street turns slightly right and becomes Pequot Road. Travel for another mile and then take a slight right onto Booth's Quarry Road. The destination is on your right with a parking area. GPS: N44 3.156', W68 48.354'

THE HIKE

On the small island of Vinalhaven resides a quiet haven of freshwater and a quaint town along with it. The town of Vinalhaven is reason enough to pay a visit to this island if you're up in the vicinity of mid-coast Maine. But the real treat is the freshwater-fed quarry called Booth's Quarry.

It was originally called Pequoit Quarry, but locals always called it Booth's Quarry due to the Booth Brothers, who owned the quarry operations, and the name stuck. In just three years, this quarry produced three million pavers for Boston, New York, and Philadelphia. It wasn't until the 1970s that this place was rediscovered and used as an epic swimming hole.

When you get to the parking lot for Booth's Quarry, head down any of the stone steps that lead you to the quarry's edge. Surrounding the swimming hole are granite ledges that jut out into the water, perfect for those who want to cool off but don't want to get

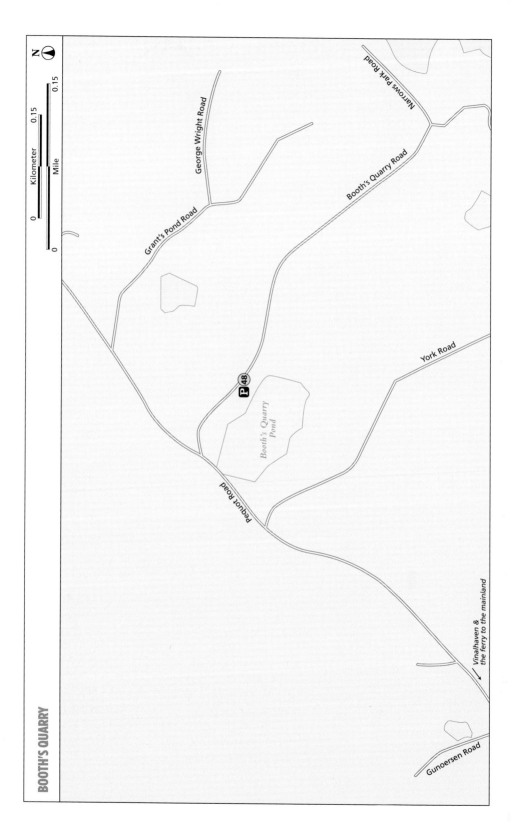

BOOTH'S QUARRY

all the way in. There are also several slabs that are not in the water, ideal for those wanting to sunbathe while the rest of their party swims.

There are some areas where folks have placed granite slabs on top of one another to create benches and picnic areas. Grass has started to work its way through the slits between the granite rocks, which is slightly more comfortable on your feet.

When you're swimming in the quarry, you'll notice it's significantly warmer than swimming in the Atlantic Ocean, which is just southeast of where the quarry sits. If you're feeling adventurous and swim out to the middle of the quarry, you might find a granite column that's only 4 feet below the surface, where you can stand up in the middle of the water. People will think you are a magician. Enjoy your time while you're at the quarry, and make sure to pick up after yourself, as there are no facilities here.

Booth's Quarry is my choice swimming hole when visiting Vinalhaven, but there is also another one on the island. It tends to be a little more popular since it's slightly closer to the ferry terminal. To get to Lawson's Quarry from the ferry, head northeast on West Main Street and then turn left on Sands Road. After 0.4 mile, turn right onto Dog Town Road/Harbor Road. After 0.3 mile, this road turns into North Haven Road. Another 0.5 mile will bring you to Lawson's Quarry.

Much like Booth's Quarry, Lawson's is filled with freshwater that is slightly warmer than the surrounding oceanic water. It also has a slightly more greenish hue to the water but is just as clean as Booth's Quarry. It's surrounded by many pine trees growing out of the slabs of rock that make up the edges of the quarry.

MILES AND DIRECTIONS

0.00 Start at the parking lot north of Booth's Quarry and work your way down to the water's edge.

Reminders not to bathe in the water HOLLY CURTIS

49 MOOSEHEAD LAKE

There are several spots to jump into Moosehead Lake, including Pebble Beach (see hike 43). But I find the best place to get the full experience of Moosehead Lake is to head to Lily Bay State Park and do the Rowell Cove and Dunn Point Trails. This state park is one of the most remote in the state, which means there aren't nearly the crowds that other state parks get. Plus, you can also choose from hiking, fishing, boating, sunbathing, kayaking, canoeing, or simply playing on the playground.

Start: At the Dunn Point trailhead
Elevation gain: 180 feet
Distance: 4.5 miles out and back
Difficulty: Easy
Hiking time: About 2 hours
Fees and permits: Fee required
Trail contact: Lily Bay State Park, 13 Myrles Way, Greenville, ME 04441; (207) 695-2700; https://apps.web .maine.gov/lilybay
Dog-friendly: Allowed on leash
Trail surface: Gravel, dirt, and pavement

Land status: Maine Bureau of Parks and Lands
Nearest town: Greenville, ME
Other trail users: Snowmobilers and cross-country skiers
Temperature of water: 60°F
Body of water: Moosehead Lake
Water availability: None
Maps: Lily Bay State Park trail map
Toilets: Yes, at the trailhead
Wheelchair compatibility: Only to the beach area at the trailhead
Family-friendly: Yes

FINDING THE TRAILHEAD

From Bangor, take ME-15 North for approximately 36 miles. When you reach Dover-Foxcroft, turn left onto ME-6 West for 8 miles and then turn right to continue on ME-6 West for another 25.6 miles. The road will turn into Lily Bay Road. Follow that road for approximately 9 miles and then turn left onto State Park Road. Follow State Park Road until you reach the end; park next to the playground and beach area. GPS: N45 34.1934', W69 33.9786'

THE HIKE

This hike was one of my loveliest surprises of finding great swimming holes to put in this book. It's so far out there that not many people visit this area and would rather take a boat out on Moosehead Lake. But this spot also has a great campground, so you can stay longer if you enjoy it.

Lily Bay State Park lies on the shores of Moosehead Lake. Due to its proximity to Pebble Beach, this is a great option to do either before or after your hike/swim up there. It's a shame to drive all this way and not have more than one hike planned for the area.

Like with many trails in this guide, you can choose to just go directly to the beach or take a little hike prior so you can get your heart pumping. If you choose the latter, start the hike along Dunn Point. The parking lot at the gravel beach and playground is the better spot to start and end your hike rather than in Rowell Cove. The trail begins on the north side of the parking lot opposite the playground. Start walking along Dunn Point Trail until you hit the road that loops around the campground. You will continue straight through until you hit the road again and hang a right.

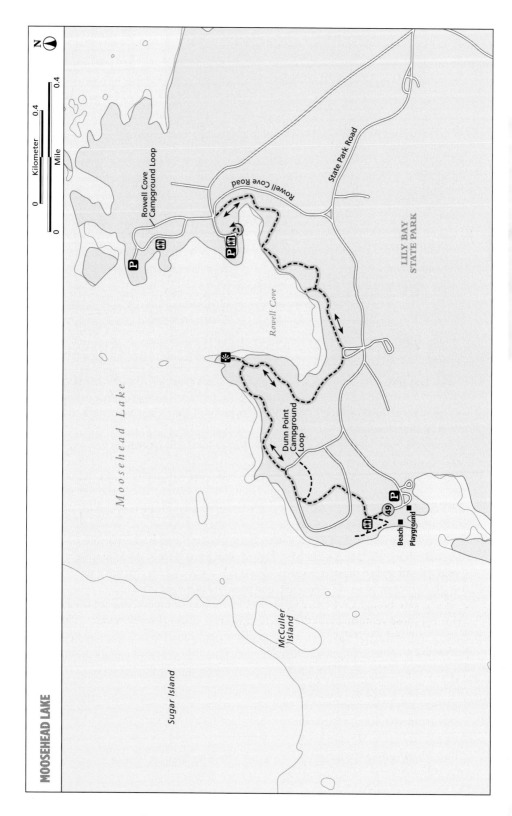

MOOSEHEAD LAKE

N

Kilometer
0   0.4

Mile
0   0.4

Moosehead Lake

Sugar Island

McCuller Island

Rowell Cove Campground Loop

Rowell Cove

Rowell Cove Road

State Park Road

LILY BAY STATE PARK

Dunn Point Campground Loop

Beach
Playground

49

P

Heading through the campground at Dunn Point will be the only time you aren't close to the shores of Moosehead Lake. Most of the trail skirts the edges of the water, where you can be in constant view of the enormity of the lake. Take a left to stay on the trail after you have walked along the campground road for 0.1 mile. In just under another 0.5 mile, there is a beautiful overlook to your left. Continue on the trail after you've taken in the views.

Once you've been on the trail for about 1.5 miles, the trail will turn into Rowell Cove Trail. Another mile will bring you to the end of Rowell Cove, where you will likely see folks launching their boats or fishing on the shores. When you are ready, go back the way you came to return to Dunn Point.

When you arrive back at Dunn Point, grab the beach accessories from your car and set up camp along the gravel beach just west of where you parked. Despite the gravel, the ground is soft and comfortable. What is truly great about a gravel beach is the lack of sand that always seems to get in your food when you are at a regular beach.

If you have brought any water equipment like kayaks or canoes, you can launch them here. For those venturing into the waters to swim, consider yourself warned. The water is very cold and could shock anyone who might not be used to it. Make sure to wade in rather than running in so your body can slowly become accustomed to the cold.

MILES AND DIRECTIONS

0.00 Start on the Dunn Point Trail to the north of the parking lot.

0.05 Stay right to continue on Dunn Point Trail.

0.10 Cross Dunn Point Road. You'll be walking through the campground.

0.30   Cross Dunn Point Road again (it's a loop) and take a right.

0.40   Take a left to stay on the trail.

0.80   Reach an overlook of Moosehead Lake.

1.30   Stay straight to continue onto Rowell Cove Trail.

2.25   Reach the northern end of Rowell Cove. Return the way you came.

3.20   Stay straight to get back on the Dunn Point Trail.

4.10   Turn right to stay on the trail.

4.20   Take a left to head back through the campground.

4.40   Cross Dunn Point Road again.

4.50   Arrive back at the trailhead.

Looking across the enormous lake

50 BLUEBERRY LEDGES

If remote is what you're after, taking the drive up to Baxter State Park should be on your must-do list. This is about as wild as it gets in New England. As a matter of fact, the start of this trail is also the beginning of the 100 Mile Wilderness along the Appalachian Trail. It's the most secluded part of the 2,190-plus-mile trek along the eastern United States. Although there might not be a lot of people, there is plenty of wildlife to make up for it.

Start: East of Abol Bridge Campground and Store at the Appalachian trailhead
Elevation gain: 340 feet
Distance: 3.8 miles out and back
Difficulty: Moderate
Hiking time: About 2 hours
Fees and permits: Fee required
Trail contact: Baxter State Park, Millinocket, ME 04462; (207) 723-5140; https://baxterstatepark.org
Dog-friendly: Not allowed
Trail surface: Gravel and dirt

Land status: Maine Bureau of Parks and Lands
Nearest town: Millinocket, ME
Other trail users: None
Temperature of water: 55°F
Body of water: Katahdin Stream
Water availability: At the campground store
Maps: Baxter State Park trail map
Toilets: Yes, at the campground store
Wheelchair compatibility: No
Family-friendly: Yes

FINDING THE TRAILHEAD

From Bangor, take I-95 North for approximately 58 miles. Take the exit for ME-157 West. Turn left and drive on ME-157 West for 11 miles and then turn right onto Katahdin Avenue. Take an immediate left at the second cross street onto Bates Street for just under 1 mile. Continue on Millinocket Road for about 6 miles, which then turns into Millinocket Lake Road for 1 mile. Continue on Baxter Park Road for 3 miles, then turn left and make an immediate right onto Golden Road. Parking will be on your left before you hit the Abol Bridge Campground and Store. GPS: N45 50.0982', W68 57.5514'

THE HIKE

Due to its remoteness, the dirt road to get to the trailhead is covered with potholes and other debris. You might even think you're going the wrong way but, trust me, you are not. This road closes in the winter due to its lack of use and remoteness, which is lucky for you since you'll only be visiting in the summertime to enjoy the water.

Start the trail by walking along the road that goes away from the Abol Bridge Campground and Store. If you need to stock up on any snacks or water, do so here. Turn left down a forest road. You will see a sign that states you are on the Appalachian Trail and 0.2 mile from the boundary of Baxter State Park.

At the small parking area at the end of this forest road, continue straight to stay on the Appalachian Trail and follow the signs for Blueberry Ledges. Cross over a small stream and take a look to your right where you can view Mount Katahdin standing prominently. When the trail forks, stay right to get off the Appalachian Trail and onto Abol Pond Trail.

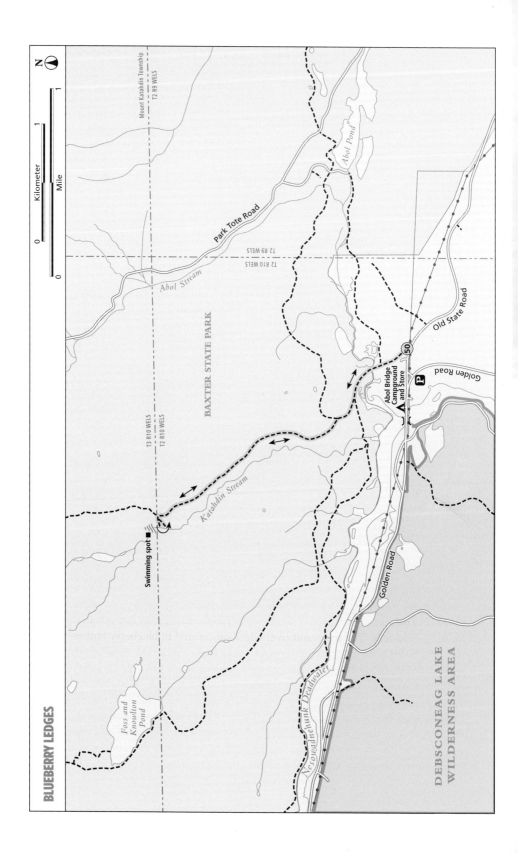

BLUEBERRY LEDGES

N

Kilometer
0   1

Mile
0   1

Mount Katahdin Township
T2 R9 WELS

Abol Pond

Park Tote Road

Abol Stream

T2 R9 WELS
T2 R10 WELS

BAXTER STATE PARK

Old State Road

Abol Bridge
Campground
and Store

50

Golden Road

P

T3 R10 WELS
T2 R10 WELS

Katahdin Stream

Swimming spot

Golden Road

Foss and
Knowlton Pond

Nesowadnehunk Deadwater

DEBSCONEAG LAKE
WILDERNESS AREA

Stay left at the next fork to get on the official trail for Blueberry Ledges and slowly make your way up the gradual ascent. If you do this hike during the week, you likely won't see a lot of folks on the trail. I went midweek and saw zero people on the way in and out. This is usually a nice reprieve for me, with my usual hiking spots always being so popular, but I'll admit this trail had me wary. I had stopped at the campground and talked with the host, who informed me that there was a lot of bear activity in the area. Luckily, I always carry bear spray with me, so I was prepared for a potential encounter. This is why it's always nice to stop in at the visitor centers and campgrounds—the locals truly do know the area best.

For me, the best way to repel bears is with my singing—it's loud and off-key. So that's exactly what I did for the majority of the trail. There were signs of recent bear activity, including several clumps of scat filled with berries and seeds.

Just after 1 mile from the last fork, you will reach a large rock cairn that indicates a turn in the trail. Head left to hike down to the waterfalls that make up Blueberry Ledges. Stay on the rock face and do not trample any of the sensitive plants and lichens that grow within the crevices. The rocks and river edges are covered in blueberry bushes—hence the name "Blueberry Ledges." There could potentially be some bear activity here due to the plethora of blueberry bushes. Stay on extra alert, since bears likely won't hear you over the roaring cascades.

When you make your way down to the river, you'll see several cascades and natural waterslides heading down the stream. You can simply sit at the water's edge and dip your toes or plunge all the way into the pool below the cascades, swimming until you're ready to head back out.

WHAT TO DO IN CASE OF A BEAR ENCOUNTER

Due to the higher likelihood of encountering a bear on this trail than other trails in this guide, here is a rundown on what to do if you see a black bear (note that grizzlies do not live in Maine or in the northeast United States). If you have kids with you, make sure you talk to them prior to any hike about the wildlife you might encounter so that they know what to do in different situations.

- First, stay calm and say hello to the bear in a calm, but strong voice. Try not to startle it. Do *not* run.
- Say something like, "Hey bear, I'm just passing through—I don't mean you any harm."
- Check your deterrent (bear spray) and have it handy in case things go sour.
- If you are downhill from a bear, try to find a spot that has higher ground. Make yourself look as big as possible.
- If the bear is stationary and not walking away, simply back away slowly. (Do so sideways to avoid tripping).
- If the bear starts to walk toward you, stop moving and stand your ground. Start yelling, waving your hands and your trekking poles. If it continues to move forward, you are welcome to throw things at it.
- Whatever you do, do *not* run and do *not* climb trees—black bears will chase you and can easily climb trees.

Although extremely rare, if you get attacked by a black bear:

- Use your bear spray when it charges you. Wait until the bear is close enough for it to be a deterrent.
- *Do not play dead.* Contrary to popular belief, playing dead will not save you in the case of a black bear attack.
- Protect your kid as much as you can and fight back, focusing your blows to the face and muzzle. Do not stop fighting for as long as you can.

But it's important to note that no one has ever been killed by a black bear in Maine in recorded history.

MILES AND DIRECTIONS

0.00 Head right along the gravel road across from the parking area (away from the store). Turn left onto the Appalachian Trail, which starts on a forest road.

0.20 Take a look to your right to take in the views of Mount Katahdin.

0.40 Veer right at the fork to get on Abol Pond Trail.

0.60 Take a left at the fork onto Blueberry Ledges Trail.

1.80 Take a left to head down to Blueberry Ledges.

1.90 Reach Blueberry Ledges and the cascading river. Turn around and return the way you came.

2.00 Take a right to head back along Blueberry Ledges Trail.

Blueberry Ledges has a series of cascades and pools

3.20   Stay straight to get back on Abol Pond Trail.

3.40   Stay straight to get back on the Appalachian Trail.

3.80   Arrive back at the trailhead.

Rattle River Falls in New Hampshire

Sculptured Rocks in
New Hampshire

THE TEN ESSENTIALS OF HIKING

American Hiking Society recommends you pack the "Ten Essentials" every time you head out for a hike. Whether you plan to be gone for a couple of hours or several months, make sure to pack these items. Become familiar with these items and know how to use them.

1. Appropriate Footwear
Happy feet make for pleasant hiking. Think about traction, support, and protection when selecting well-fitting shoes or boots.

2. Navigation
While phones and GPS units are handy, they aren't always reliable in the backcountry; consider carrying a paper map and compass as a backup and know how to use them.

3. Water (and a way to purify it)
As a guideline, plan for half a liter of water per hour in moderate temperatures/terrain. Carry enough water for your trip and know where and how to treat water while you're out on the trail.

4. Food
Pack calorie-dense foods to help fuel your hike, and carry an extra portion in case you are out longer than expected.

5. Rain Gear & Dry-Fast Layers
The weatherman is not always right. Dress in layers to adjust to changing weather and activity levels. Wear moisture-wicking cloths and carry a warm hat.

6. Safety Items (light, fire, and a whistle)
Have means to start an emergency fire, signal for help, and see the trail and your map in the dark.

7. First Aid Kit

Supplies to treat illness or injury are only as helpful as your knowledge of how to use them. Take a class to gain the skills needed to administer first aid and CPR.

8. Knife or Multi-Tool

With countless uses, a multi-tool can help with gear repair and first aid.

9. Sun Protection

Sunscreen, sunglasses, and sun-protective clothing should be used in every season regardless of temperature or cloud cover.

10. Shelter

Protection from the elements in the event you are injured or stranded is necessary. A lightweight, inexpensive space blanket is a great option.

Find other helpful resources at AmericanHiking.org/hiking-resources